Re-envisioning the Literacy Block

How do you ensure you're using literacy instruction effectively to meet the needs of all of your students? In this book from Diana and Betsy Sisson, you'll learn an innovative approach to using the literacy block in a gradual release model that allows you to provide grade-appropriate teaching as well as meaningful, individualized instruction to close the academic gaps of struggling learners and offer accelerated experiences for advanced students.

What's inside:

- Part I of the book lays out the authors' framework for the Core Block.
- Part II explains how to use the re-envisioned block to integrate the core components of word study, vocabulary development, strategic reading instruction, writers' craft, and expanded reading opportunities.
- Part III reveals how to use differentiation, project-based learning, and assessment to prepare students for new literacy demands.
- The appendix provides literacy block schedules, tools for phonics development and morphology study, and correlations to the Common Core.

Each chapter includes practical tools and examples, as well as "In Action" scenarios to show how the ideas look in an authentic classroom.

Diana Sisson and **Betsy Sisson** are international literacy consultants focusing on professional development and school improvement. They also serve as adjunct professors in the fields of teacher preparation, curriculum and instruction, research in literacy, and special educational programming.

Other Eye On Education Books Available from Routledge
(www.routledge.com/eyeoneducation)

**Close Reading in Elementary School:
Bringing Readers and Texts Together**
Diana Sisson and Betsy Sisson

**The Common Core Grammar Toolkit:
Using Mentor Texts to Teach the Language
Standards in Grades 3–5**
Sean Ruday

**The Informational Writing Toolkit:
Using Mentor Texts in Grades 3–5**
Sean Ruday

**Infusing Grammar into the Writer's Workshop:
A Guide for K–6 Teachers**
Amy Benjamin and Barbara Golub

**Writing Strategies That Work:
Do This—Not That!**
Lori G. Wilfong

**Nonfiction Strategies That Work:
Do This—Not That!**
Lori G. Wilfong

**Vocabulary Strategies That Work:
Do This—Not That!**
Lori G. Wilfong

**Math Workshop in Action:
Strategies for Grades K–5**
Nicki Newton

**Guided Math in Action:
Building Each Student's Mathematical Proficiency
with Small-Group Instruction**
Nicki Newton

Re-envisioning the Literacy Block

A Guide to Maximizing Instruction in Grades K–8

Diana Sisson and Betsy Sisson

Routledge
Taylor & Francis Group
NEW YORK AND LONDON

First published 2016
by Routledge
711 Third Avenue, New York, NY 10017

and by Routledge
2 Park Square, Milton Park, Abingdon, Oxon OX14 4RN

*Routledge is an imprint of the Taylor & Francis Group,
an informa business*

© 2016 Taylor & Francis

The right of Diana Sisson and Betsy Sisson to be identified as
authors of this work has been asserted by them in accordance
with sections 77 and 78 of the Copyright, Designs and Patents
Act 1988.

All rights reserved. No part of this book may be reprinted or
reproduced or utilised in any form or by any electronic,
mechanical, or other means, now known or hereafter invented,
including photocopying and recording, or in any information
storage or retrieval system, without permission in writing from
the publishers.

The URLs in this book were current at the time of publication
but are subject to change.

Trademark notice: Product or corporate names may be
trademarks or registered trademarks, and are used only for
identification and explanation without intent to infringe.

Library of Congress Cataloging in Publication Data
Sisson, Diana.
  Re-envisioning the literacy block : a guide to maximizing
instruction in grades K-8 / by Diana Sisson and Betsy Sisson.
      pages cm
  Includes bibliographical references.
  1. Language arts (Elementary) 2. Language arts (Middle
school) 3. Literacy. I. Sisson, Betsy. II. Title.
  LB1576.S48 2016
  372.6—dc23
  2015013032

ISBN: 978-1-138-90352-4 (hbk)
ISBN: 978-1-138-90353-1 (pbk)
ISBN: 978-1-315-69686-7 (ebk)

Typeset in Palatino
by Apex CoVantage, LLC

Dedication

To our book club friends, Eileen, Jackie, Joanne, Kathy, and Sandy.

Despite our monthly ritual of selecting a book, our time together usually becomes an opportunity for us to see one another, eat amazing food, and talk about education. We may not be a traditional book club, but we wouldn't have it any other way.

Contents

Preface xi
Meet the Authors xv

Part I: Foundations of Literacy Instruction

1   Historical Trends in Literacy Instruction 3
Brief History of Reading Methodology 4
Origins of the Literacy Block and Guided Reading 6
Benefits and Challenges of the Literacy Block 7
Conclusion 9

2   The Core Block 11
Gradual Release of Responsibility Instructional Model . . .12
Overview of Components in the Core Block 17
Guided Reading 23
Small-Group Application 27
The Core Block "In Action" 28
Conclusion 30

Part II: Components of the Core Block

3   Word Study 33
Significance of Word Study for Literacy Achievement 36
Phonemic Awareness 39
Phonics Development 41
Morphology 45
Word Study "In Action" 50
Conclusion 54

4   Vocabulary Development 55
Significance of Vocabulary for Literacy Achievement 55
Key Principles for Robust Vocabulary Acquisition 57
Personalized Vocabulary Study 61

viii ◆ Contents

Vocabulary APP Centers. 64
Vocabulary "In Action". 72
Conclusion 74

5   **Strategic Reading Instruction** 75
Significance of Comprehension for Literacy
    Achievement 75
Comprehension APP Centers 78
Universal Comprehension Strategy Instruction 83
Standards-Based Strategy Instruction 84
Prescriptive Strategy Instruction. 84
Integrated Strategy Instruction 85
Fluency's Role in Comprehending Text 87
Comprehension Strategies "In Action" 94
Conclusion 98

6   **Writers' Craft.** 99
Significance of Writers' Craft for Literacy Achievement . . .100
The Reading-Writing Connection .101
Integrating Writing Instruction in the Classroom. 104
Writers' Craft "In Action" 112
Conclusion 114

7   **Expanded Reading Opportunities** 115
Significance of Expanded Time for Student Reading
    on Literacy Achievement 116
Read Aloud. 118
Independent Reading 120
Book Groups. 123
Extended Reading Opportunities "In Action" 124
Conclusion 128

Part III: Ensuring Student Success

8   **Differentiating Instruction.** 131
Individualizing Instruction for Students 134
Content 135
Process. 137

Product 142
Conclusion 143

9 Project-Based Learning 145
What Is Project-Based Learning? 146
The Power of Project-Based Learning 148
Misconceptions about Project-Based Learning 149
Obstacles in Implementing Project-Based Learning 151
Integration of Projects into the Literacy Block 152
Suggested PBL Study Topics 155
Conclusion 155

10 Assessment 159
Attributes of Effective Assessment .161
Varied Means of Assessment 167
Conclusion 175

Appendices
   Appendix A—Literacy Block Schedules 179
   Appendix B—Phonics Development 181
   Appendix C—Morphology Study 185
   Appendix D—Common Core Standards 195
References 213

Preface

In 2006, *Time* magazine ran a cover story titled "How to Bring Our Schools Out of the 20th Century," which included a passage that captures the essence of why we felt compelled to write this book.

> There's a dark little joke exchanged by educators with a dissident streak. Rip Van Winkle awakens in the 21st century after a hundred-year snooze and is, of course, utterly bewildered by what he sees. Men and women dash about, talking to small metal devices pinned to their ears. Young people sit at home on sofas, moving miniature athletes around on electronic screens. Older folk defy death and disability with metronomes in their chests and with hips made of metal and plastic. Airports, hospitals, shopping malls—every place that Rip goes just baffles him. But when he finally walks into a schoolroom, the old man knows exactly where he is. "This is a school," he declares. "We used to have these back in 1906. Only now the blackboards are green." (Wallis & Steptoe, 2006, p. 50)

We have devoted our professional lives to literacy—in public schools and private schools, at K–12 settings and university campuses, through classroom teaching and instructional coaching, and both nationally and internationally. In these varied roles, we have worked with students from pre-kindergarten to adults, and what remains indisputable is that the greatest concerns stem from the literacy needs of K–8 students.

We see this everyday with our work with educators. The most common question we encounter centers on how we, as a profession, can ensure young learners acquire the literacy skills necessary to become independent readers and writers. Commercial programs abound. Literacy models are thriving. Books devoted to literacy instruction have reached record levels. Yet, despite all of these resources and the valiant efforts of teachers, students are struggling. We believe that part of the disconnect originates from the literacy block itself.

In the last two decades, we have witnessed the gamut of literacy instruction designs. Some schools have no protected block of time for literacy. Others have a literacy block incorporated in their daily schedule but grapple with what to include and how to teach it. Still others have an effective literacy block for some but worry that they are providing enough support for their struggling learners or sufficient acceleration for advanced students.

We strongly believe that the literacy block has the potential to transform your instruction and ultimately the literacy development of your students. To do this, the block must reflect an emphasis on balanced literacy, an awareness of the sequential development of core skills, an integration of explicit and prescriptive instruction, and a gradual release of responsibility that ensures that students receive the necessary scaffolding to enable them to become successful.

We embedded these elements into a literacy block model we designed several years ago and have since used across kindergarten to eighth grade. Our vision of effective instruction revolved around a core set of learning goals for all students along with targeted, prescriptive learning goals for individual students—be it remediation or enrichment. Because of the power core learning goals hold to alter the paradigm of literacy instruction, we called our model the Core Block.

The Core Block divides literacy instruction into three distinct, yet overlapping, components. Teachers offer whole-group instruction, guided reading, and small-group application. Within each of these sections, "core knowledge" is embedded and strengthened. This core knowledge emerges from a balanced literacy philosophy so that learning focuses on phonological awareness, phonics, vocabulary, comprehension, and fluency. How is this different from other literacy block models? First, it doesn't require a commercial program or script. It depends on teacher expertise and customized learning aligned to the needs of each student. Second, it doesn't just address balanced literacy;

balanced literacy forms the bedrock of instruction. Third, rather than delivering a generic program, the Core Block applies itself to the literacy development of the entire class and then targets the specific learning needs of each individual, ensuring equitable educational opportunities for every student.

As we have worked with teachers to utilize the Core Block in their classrooms, we have observed their transition to more focused, structured teaching. They have verbalized how this model has made teaching and assessing easier and more responsive to student needs. Likewise, students have demonstrated a more positive self-image of themselves as readers and voiced their belief that their reading and writing have improved. Special needs educators have suggested that this model offered their students the most support they had ever received in the general education classroom. Ultimately, student achievement scores increased as teaching and learning converged on the core knowledge that we expect our students to master.

In this book, we hope to share with you how to develop the Core Block and implement it in your own classroom with ease and fidelity. Along the way, we will explain how writing can become an integral part of your literacy block, how differentiation can and should be incorporated every day, and what effective assessment looks like in today's classroom.

The demands placed on education may have evolved since 1906, but our instructional practice has not. Look around your school, your classroom. Little has changed. This book is about how to awaken your instructional practice to tackle the challenges that we all must meet.

The literacy block has had many iterations over the past few decades. Each of them is characterized by its unique strengths and weaknesses. None of them, however, offers comprehensive prescriptive instruction. None of them ensures educational equity for all students. None of them fuses the literacy block together around core knowledge that every student should possess. We believe that the Core Block addresses these deficits and provides a systematic instructional model that makes certain all students succeed . . . and thrive.

Meet the Authors

Dr. Diana Sisson and **Dr. Betsy Sisson** hold doctorates in educational leadership and policy studies as well as being certified reading consultants with a combined experience of over 30 years. The sisters have worked abroad in developing reading programs for students in international settings, consulted on federal research grants, presented at national and international conferences, and guest lectured at a number of universities. They currently work as reading consultants, serve as adjunct professors at Central Connecticut State University and the University of Saint Joseph in literacy, special education, and educational research, as well as operate their own consulting company focusing on school improvement and professional development services.

Their professional publications center on equitable educational opportunities for all students. In addition to this book, they have written three others texts: *Close Reading in Elementary School—Bringing Readers and Texts Together* (Routledge, 2014), *Targeted Reading Interventions for the Common Core Classroom—Tested Lessons That Help Struggling Students Meet the Rigors of the Standards—K–3* (Scholastic, 2014), and *Targeted Reading Interventions for the Common Core Classroom—Tested Lessons That Help Struggling Students Meet the Rigors of the Standards—4 and Up* (Scholastic, 2014).

Diana and Betsy also sit on the board of the Connecticut Association for Reading Research (CARR). In their capacity as research chairs for CARR, they are undertaking a study delving into teacher preparation programs in the field of literacy.

Part I
Foundations of Literacy Instruction

- Historical Trends in Literacy Instruction
- The Core Block

1

Historical Trends in Literacy Instruction

Reading. It was invented only a few thousand years ago. Quintilian, the renowned Roman educator from the 1st century, spoke of wooden tablets filled with letters used to teach students how to read. The first reading book, the primer, became popular in the Middle Ages and was encouraged by the Church to ensure children learned key Biblical texts, such as the Lord's Prayer and the Ten Commandments. As English settlers began to travel to the New World that would some day become the United States, they brought these religious convictions with them, instructing students not only on how to read, but also on their society, their culture, and their beliefs. What remained consistent throughout all of this was the methodology of how students learned to read. For over 2,000 years, reading instruction centered on the alphabetic principle, or phonics, approach. What had been unswerving in the past has undergone radical upheaval in the last century and a half. As we now move into a dramatically different landscape of technologically driven societies and increased demands for highly literate citizens, reading methodology has come under intense scrutiny. It leads to only one conclusion: the way we prepare

> "Reading was the most important subject in our early American schools, and it has continued to be the most important subject all through the years of our national growth."
>
> *(Smith, 2002, p. xv)*

students for 21st century demands must change. Nothing explains that need more than a look back at the prevailing thoughts from past decades and how they continue to shape the future of reading instruction.

Brief History of Reading Methodology

In the colonial period of the United States, instruction centered on the alphabetic approach, and students were directed toward reading texts, such as the Bible and the Horn Book, and later the New England Primer. Little thought was given to any other method. Instruction was dominated by learning the alphabet, recitation of letter names and syllables, memorization, spelling bees, and oral reading.

Around the middle of the 19th century, significant change came into classrooms. Horace Mann, the Secretary of the Massachusetts State Board of Education, began to argue that breaking down words into constituent parts using the sound–symbol relationship was simply too difficult for young children, and the texts used to learn to read were meaningless; instead, he advocated for a "whole word" approach. Students also began to read from the McGuffy Readers, which included stories designed to interest children, pre-reading activities, and a focus on comprehension, and became the forerunner of the modern-day basal series.

In the 1930s, Dick and Jane leveled readers, with their repetitive "look-say" controlled vocabulary approach, became a mainstay in classrooms. They included teacher guides, scripted lessons, and word lists. Emphasizing sight words and comprehension, they generally excluded the previous code-based, alphabetic approach. During this time, students were urged to use picture or context clues to determine meaning.

In 1955, Rudolph Flesch penned the highly controversial *Why Johnny Can't Read* in which he renounced the look-say method, arguing against the use of the Dick and Jane readers. In contrast, he made the case that phonics was the most effective method to teach reading and that students should not be denied instruction in how to break the alphabetic code, emphasizing

> Ever since 1500 B.C.—wherever an alphabetic system of writing was used—people have learned to read by simply memorizing the sound of each letter in their alphabet. . . . The ancient Egyptians learned that way, and the Greeks and the Romans, and the French and the Germans, and the Dutch and the Portuguese, and the Turks and the Bulgarians and the Estonians and the Icelanders and the Abyssinians—every single nation throughout history that used an alphabetic system of writing. (1955/1986, p. ix/p. 5)

By the 1970s, however, proponents of the whole language movement rejected what they deemed the "drill and kill" phonics worksheets commonly found in the ubiquitous basal series that had become the dominant form of instruction in American classrooms. In their place came the return to the whole-word, or meaning-based, approach. Rejecting the belief that word analysis through phonics is the best way to teach reading, they supported the notion that a child learns to read through meaningful, authentic contexts. Similarly, the Transactional Theory, which espoused the conviction that meaning is constructed only by the interaction between the text and reader, gained national prominence in the educational field. Meanwhile, commercial programs became the bedrock of instruction in classrooms to such a degree that Shannon (1989) declared that "the roles of teacher and textbook seem to be reversed . . . wherein teachers become a support system for the textbook rather than the other way around" (p. xiv).

These highly contentious times, which polarized the reading field, are commonly known as the "Reading Wars." In the midst of the debate swirling among reading educators and researchers, large-scale national studies attempted to address the controversy. In a 1975 National Institute of Education report, Chall made the case that neither phonics nor the look-say approach was sufficient by themselves, and the 1998 National Reading Council suggested that the two approaches should be integrated. Finally, the 2000 National Reading Panel report brought the concept of *balanced literacy* to the nation's attention, encouraging educators to capitalize on the best of both philosophies—systematic, explicit instruction on sound–symbol relationships coupled with ongoing opportunities to apply those skills in authentic texts—through five key pillars of effective instruction: phonemic awareness, phonics, vocabulary, fluency, and comprehension.

While it may seem to have heralded the end of an era of pendulum swings in reading methodology, the current acceptance of balanced literacy embodies its own difficulties. Balanced instruction may sound as simple as combining two opposing philosophies; it is actually much more complicated. Cowen (2003) reminds us that

> effective balanced literacy instruction requires a very comprehensive, integrated approach, demanding that teachers know a great deal about literacy research related to emergent literacy, assessment-based instruction, phonological and phonemic awareness, the alphabetic principle, phonics and word study, selecting appropriate leveled readers, reader response, writing process, and constructivist learning. (p. 2)

So the war may be over, but the battle for effective literacy instruction continues. Ask yourself these questions: Do you have a balanced literacy program? What makes it so? Do you feel confident in your abilities to "balance" instruction in such a way that students truly reap the benefits from both philosophies? These concerns can be resolved in a well-designed literacy block—one that also addresses the needs and demands of the 21st century.

Origins of the Literacy Block and Guided Reading

The literacy block and guided reading, in some form, have been discussed, implemented, and reviewed for decades. In the classic 1946 text, *Foundations of Reading Instruction*, Emmett Betts wrote about "directed reading activities," which incorporated building background knowledge, motivating students to engage with the text, guiding a first round of silent reading, focusing on word recognition skills and comprehension, rereading (either orally or silent), and then concluding with follow-up activities to "encourage the pupils to apply and extend skills, ability, and information gained from the directed reading activity" (p. 517). Doesn't this sound remarkably like a literacy block with guided reading and learning centers?

The term, *guided reading*, was actually used in print in Lillian Gray and Dora Reese's 1957 text, *Teaching Children to Read*, in which they listed the four steps within a lesson to include— preparing for the story, guided reading, skills and drills, and follow-up activities. Although they divided the times to complete literacy instruction throughout the day, they allotted a total of nearly two hours to concentrated reading work.

Despite these early models, it would be Myrtle Simpson and Ruth Trevor, literacy educators from New Zealand, who would pioneer guided reading in the 1960s. They later shared their work in part of a 1972 New Zealand handbook titled *Suggestions for Teaching Reading in Primary and Secondary Schools*. After securing the rights to a series of leveled books from New Zealand, Tom Wright from the Wright Group brought guided reading into American classrooms. Today, the practice of guided reading has flourished and has become an established literacy practice found in "thousands of classrooms around the world" (Fountas & Pinnell, 2012, p. 268), and the literacy block has become a recognized structure in classroom scheduling.

Benefits and Challenges of the Literacy Block

The advent of balanced literacy brought questions beyond how well it meshed two such opposing philosophies. The issue became, Is a balanced literacy model actually effective? Can it increase student achievement? A number of studies reveal that when a balanced literacy approach is implemented, students show marked growth in standardized measures (Bitter, O'Day,

Gubbins, & Socias, 2009; French, Morgan, Vanayan, & White, 2001). The use of centers within the literacy block has also been found to be instrumental in student learning (Burke & Baillie, 2011; Maurer, 2010).

Indeed, reading experiences of all kinds are important to students' literacy development, but they each serve a different purpose. Read alouds permit students to experience texts that they may not yet read independently. Shared reading models the skills and strategies of proficient readers. It is guided reading, though, when teachers support students' efforts to utilize strategies and skills with authentic text.

At the very heart of guided reading, students read aloud to a teacher, and the teacher provides explicit instruction, correction, and feedback to scaffold reading proficiency. The strength of guided reading comes from opportunities to provide structured support to students as they apply intentional strategies to construct meaning from text. Not surprisingly, Ford and Opitz (2011) reason that the term *guided* speaks to the educator's role of coaching students—not simply passing on information—and refer to the work of Taylor, Pearson, Clark, and Walpole (2000) in which they state that this use of coaching during guided reading may be a primary distinguishing characteristic between modestly effective schools and extremely effective ones.

Guided reading offers a range of benefits to literacy development, and educator practitioners and researchers alike typically affirm its benefits to young learners, second-language learners, and special needs students (Avalos, Plasencia, Chavez, & Rascón, 2007; Simpson, Spencer, Button, & Rendon, 2007; Suits, 2003). It supports foundational reading and writing skills, identifies student-specific strengths and weaknesses, increases comprehension and fluency, and—if done well—creates a set of strategies students "own" that can be put to use when reading, allowing them to internalize the strategies within their own repertoire.

Sadly, while guided reading is prevalent in the primary grades, educators often believe that it is only effective for very young children. As students progress through the grades, they have less and less experiences in small-group instruction (Fletcher, Greenwood, Grimley, Parkhill, & Davis, 2012) although even in

1999 the International Reading Association (1999) released a position statement asserting that "no one is giving adolescent literacy much press. . . . Many people don't recognize reading development as a continuum" (p. 1); and yet, "adolescents deserve more than a centralized one-size-fits-all approach to literacy" (p. 8). Guided reading, then, is not simply a practice appropriate for primary classrooms, but should continue to be a foundational component for older readers, particularly those who struggle.

Conclusion

Much has changed in the reading field, and how we define effective instruction has emerged as nothing short of a metamorphosis. In the desire to ensure that your students receive the best possible reading instruction, remember one undeniable truth—a program will never be as important as good teachers in the classroom who understand literacy development and can provide prescriptive, on-the-spot support. With a balanced literacy block in place that provides personalized, rigorous teaching, you can be certain that your students are receiving the best possible education and, along the way, acquiring the competencies and experiences they need to help them become the confident, independent readers we want all of our children to become.

2

The Core Block

What characterizes effective instruction remains one of the most examined issues in education. We research it, write about it, attend conferences to discuss it; and yet we continue to ponder—what makes good teaching? While many viewpoints exist, one of the most agreed upon features is the use of a *gradual release of responsibility* as a means to increase student engagement and learning.

A gradual release of responsibility should guide instructional practice during the literacy block, and in most literacy models, there are vestiges of it, especially in planning guided reading. The Core Literacy Block, however, incorporates this instructional model as a foundational principle that drives every element of the teaching and learning process. To understand the value

> "Effective instruction often follows a progression in which teachers gradually do less of the work and students gradually assume increased responsibility for their learning. It is through this process of gradually assuming more and more responsibility for their learning that students become competent, independent learners."
> *(Graves & Fitzgerald, 2003, p. 98)*

of a gradual release of responsibility, let's look back at how it was developed, the educational theory behind it, and how it is used in today's classrooms.

Gradual Release of Responsibility Instructional Model

Pearson and Gallagher (1983) developed this model to describe the process by which educators follow a protocol of explicit instruction, followed by guided practice, and then independent application with the goal of transitioning students toward becoming self-sufficient learners. The authors explain

> when the teacher is taking all or most of the responsibility for task completion, he is "modeling" or demonstrating the desired application of some strategy. When the student is taking all or most of that responsibility, she is "practicing" or "applying" that strategy. What comes in between these two extremes is the gradual release of responsibility from teacher to student. (pp. 337–338)

This release of responsibility transitions teachers from holding "all the responsibility for performing a task. . . . to a situation in which the students assume all of the responsibility" (Duke & Pearson, 2002, p. 211).

The coining of the term *gradual release of responsibility* is credited to Pearson and Gallagher. However, their work links to previous theorists, including Piaget (1952), Vygotsky (1962/1978), Wood, Bruner, and Ross (1976), Bandura (1977), and Palinscar and Brown (1983). Figure 2.1 traces an evolutionary pathway from Vygotsky's Zone of Proximal Development and its implications for learning theory, to the Wood, Bruner, and Ross concept of scaffolding and its use in instructional practice, to Pearson and Gallagher's focus on reading instruction with the gradual release of responsibility (GRR) model.

The pathway begins with Vygotsky's theory of social interaction as a vehicle for learning and his concept of the Zone of Proximal Development (ZPD), which he characterized as the

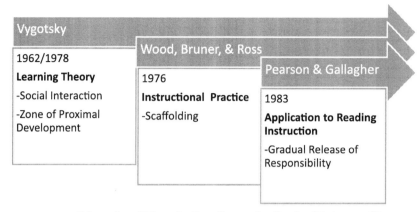

FIGURE 2.1 Educational Theories Leading to the Gradual Release of Responsibility Model

distance between the child's actual developmental level as determined by independent problem solving and the higher level of potential development as determined through problem solving under adult guidance and in collaboration with more capable peers. (1978, p. 86)

Vygotsky believed that when a student is operating within the ZPD, providing appropriate assistance will ensure that the student will be able to achieve the given task.

While Vygotsky's work centered on learning theory, Wood, Bruner, and Ross (1976) focused their work on instructional practice. Using the concept of *scaffolding*, they defined it as an "adult controlling those elements of the task that are essentially beyond the learner's capacity, thus permitting him to concentrate upon and complete only those elements that are within his range of competence" (p. 90).

Although scaffolding does not eliminate student error, its benefit is that you can utilize errors to inform your future instruction, thus personalizing learning opportunities to meet the needs of your students. Burch (2007) asserted that

> simply immersing children in literacy-rich environments is not enough to successfully offset the difficulties of

struggling readers. The most powerful tool for struggling readers is a teacher who is knowledgeable about the literacy process and is capable of constructing and providing students with supportive reading and writing opportunities that will guide them to independent, self-regulated literacy. (p. 33)

A study focusing on ELL (English language learners) reading achievement further revealed that students who received scaffolded instruction made significant gains over those who did not (Safadi & Rababah, 2012), which is critical to learning because "scaffolding is actually a bridge used to build upon what students already know to arrive at something they do not know. If scaffolding is properly administered, it will act as an enabler, not as a disabler" (Benson, 1997, p. 126). This conviction has been validated through numerous studies documenting the positive effects of scaffolding on student learning (Simons & Klein, 2007; Van de Pol, Volman, & Beishuizen, 2010; Wood & Middleon, 1975).

In 1983, Pearson and Gallagher conducted a meta-analysis centered on the review and analysis of comprehension instruction studies. They concluded that the studies they examined suggested "any academic task can be conceptualized as requiring differing proportions of teacher and student responsibility for student completion" (p. 337), positing their model of explicit instruction that would become more popularly known as the gradual release of responsibility model.

Although this framework, characterized by transitioning from teacher responsibility to student responsibility, has become a foundational principle in literacy instructional programs, there are several contemporary versions commonly found in classrooms today, including "teach-practice-apply" (Cooper, Warncke, & Shipman, 1979; Reinhartz, 1986), "to/for, with, and by" (Mooney, 1990), and "I do, we do, you do" (Campbell, 2009). While each conceptualization has its unique lens, the underlying ideology remains consistent.

Teach-Practice-Apply encourages teachers to sectionalize lessons into three specific components. During the Teach phase, the teacher introduces, presents, explains, and models a new topic or skill. Within the Practice phase, the focus shifts from teacher to students—with learners being actively engaged with the content and the teacher monitoring their progress. When satisfied that students have a reasonable grasp of the content, the teacher moves into the Apply phase and tasks students to complete work with less supervision or to attempt the skill in a different context.

In Mooney's classic 1990 text, *Reading TO, WITH, and BY Children*, she recommends that teachers read to students, with students, and by students—with each step requiring the teacher's decision as to the level of responsibility, or involvement, necessitated to meet the needs of the learners. In relationship to these phases, she highlights the practices of shared reading, guided reading, and independent reading.

Also linked to the gradual release of responsibility, the "model, lead, test" strategy (Campbell, 2009; Carnine & Silbert, 1979) is now commonly known as the "I do, we do, you do" mantra. It concentrates instruction within three steps—teaching and modeling, guided practice, and independent practice.

Looking at these iterations of the GRR model, it becomes clear that they share a fundamental aspect of instruction that centers on three distinct phases for student learning. Table 2.1 illustrates how tightly these models align with one another as well as a depiction of what may take place within each of the three phases with instructional activities, teacher actions, and student responsibilities.

Despite the appearance of Table 2.1, remember that the GRR model may not be linear. Rather, your students may shift back and forth between acquisition, scaffolding, and mastery. For example, your students may progress through an instructional loop, beginning with explicit teaching, collaboration, and independence but then start the process again as you chunk student learning, provide focused re-teaching, or even halt the release to meet the needs of the students. This can be demonstrated in a lesson on distinguishing between fact and opinion. In planning the lesson, you may elect to chunk identifying fact (teach, collaboration, independence), then circle back and teach students how to determine opinion (teach, collaboration,

16 ◆ Foundations of Literacy Instruction

TABLE 2.1 Comparison of Gradual Release of Responsibility Models

Vygotsky's Zone of ACTUAL Development			Vygotsky's Zone of PROXIMAL Development & Scaffolds			Vygotsky's Zone of POTENTIAL Development (or "New" Development)		
"Teach"			"Practice"			"Apply"		
"TO children"			"WITH children"			"BY children"		
"I do"			"We do"			"You do"		
EXPLICIT TEACHING (Acquisition of Learning)			**COLLABORATION** (Scaffolding of Learning)			**INDEPENDENCE** (Mastery of Learning)		
Instructional Activity	Teacher	Students	Instructional Activity	Teacher	Students	Instructional Activity	Teacher	Students
Direct instruction	Models	Listen	Guided reading	Checks	Work collaboratively	Independent reading	Evaluates	Apply
	Demonstrates	Participate					Offers feedback	
Read aloud		Asks questions		Prompts		Learning centers		Problem-solve
Think aloud	Explains			Clarifies				
Shared reading						Application activities		Self-correct
				Observes				
Mini-lessons						Conferences		Work independently

independence), and finally focus on how readers discern the difference between the two (teach, collaboration, independence). In a different scenario, you may .plan a lesson on a specific summarizing strategy and complete all three components of the GRR model only to discover that your students are struggling with this particular strategy. Using the student data collected, you may settle on a different summarizing strategy and re-initiate the process again. A more urgent issue may arise if you deliver instruction and your students are simply unable to transition to collaborative work due to an acute lack of understanding of the content. In this case, you may feel compelled to stop and loop back to the first phase of explicit teaching to begin again.

As illustrated in these examples, the GRR model exemplifies best practice for literacy instruction. Often associated with differentiation, it allows you to individualize targeted instruction for your students. By chunking the content and slowly fading away the support as students gain confidence, you engage and motivate them to build their academic skills in a completely supportive environment. It will also "ensure that students develop reading habits and automaticity" (Fisher & Frey, 2008, p. 17). Armed with these facts, consider the components of the Core Block and how the GRR model interlocks core knowledge in a fluid, student-centered approach to the literacy block.

Overview of Components in the Core Block

Literacy block models commonly integrate three central components: whole-group instruction, guided reading, and small-group work. As shown in Figure 2.2, the Core Block retains these basic

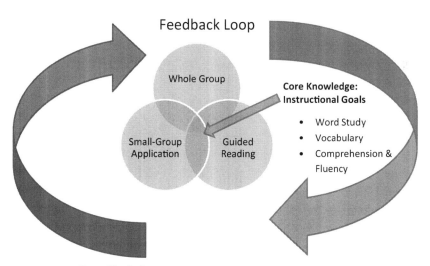

FIGURE 2.2 Core Block Overview

elements but links them together in a coordinated framework of focused teaching and learning in an ongoing feedback loop with identified instructional goals at its center.

Whole-Group Instruction. Let's consider the typical 90-minute literacy block. Start your instruction with the whole group. Rather than mini-lessons that change weekly or even daily, focus every day's whole-group time on three elements of a balanced literacy program.

1. Word Study (Phonological awareness/Phonics/Morphology)
2. Vocabulary (Foundational word list/Grade-level appropriate core word list/Accelerated word list)
3. Comprehension and Fluency (Comprehension strategies/Fluency activities)

For a 90-minute literacy block, you incorporate 30 minutes for whole-group work, providing direct instruction in word study for 10 minutes, vocabulary for 10 minutes, and comprehension for 10 minutes. (See Appendix A for other literacy block schedules, including those with 45 minutes, 60 minutes, and 120 minutes.)

This configuration serves several purposes. First, it delivers dedicated time for each of the elements of a balanced literacy program. For example, within one week's time, your students will receive nearly an hour of instruction on just word study. Over the course of a typical school year, that number catapults to 30 hours of committed, explicit instruction on each of these elements! Second, it provides evenhanded instruction so that your students use these "building blocks" collectively as they develop their literacy skills. Third, the focal points of the whole-group instruction form a roadmap for both guided reading and small-group application. Thus, what you introduce during whole group will be reinforced during the collaborative work of guided reading and strengthened during small-group application. In effect, you tie each of the components of the literacy block to the others through the instructional goals of word work, vocabulary, and comprehension and fluency.

Word Study. Word Study centers on developing students' knowledge of words through a research-based progression of layered understanding of English orthography—alphabet, pattern, and meaning (Bear, Invernizzi, Templeton, & Johnston, 2014; Invernizz & Hayes, 2004). For very young students, the alphabet layer (phonological awareness) introduces the relationship between letters and sounds. (Example: *Mat* has three sounds— m / a / t.) The pattern layer (phonics) supports the understanding that letters may have more than one sound and that patterns of letters help readers know how to pronounce words. (Example: *Mate* follows a pattern of consonant-vowel-consonant-e, which means that the vowel sound will be long and the e will be silent.) For more mature students, the meaning layer (morphology) makes use of structural analysis, groups of letters forming prefixes, suffixes, and root words. (Example: The suffix -ful in *joyful* is pronounced like the word *full* and indicates "full of joy." The reader also knows that words ending in *-ful* are adjectives so if he or she encounters an unfamiliar word, there is additional syntactical support with determining the meaning of unknown words.)

During Word Study, the teacher of a kindergarten class may deliver instruction on segmenting sounds, while a second-grade teacher focuses on r-controlled vowels. Meanwhile, students in Grade 6 may receive a lesson on root words. You determine students' placement on the progression of skills, providing appropriate instruction along a continuum of competencies. Chapter 3 includes the instructional sequence of word study as well as engaging student activities for whole-group, guided reading, and small-group application.

Vocabulary. "The importance of vocabulary in reading achievement has been recognized for more than half a century" (National Reading Panel, 2000, p. 4–15). Without a solid vocabulary base, students simply cannot comprehend text with any level of proficiency (Graves, 2009), and this manifests as early as kindergarten with vocabulary becoming the most powerful predictor of reading comprehension in the primary grades (Stahl & Nagy, 2006; Storch & Whitehurst, 2002). Chall, Jacobs, and Baldwin (1990) also established that the reading difficulties of low-income children are not predominantly hindered by

20 ◆ Foundations of Literacy Instruction

cognitive factors. Rather, the most significant stumbling block for their academic achievement and teachable literacy skills is a vocabulary deficit. In fact, the prominent researcher, E. D. Hirsch, Jr. (2003) argued that "it is now well accepted that the chief cause of the achievement gap between socioeconomic groups is a language gap" (p. 22). With such compelling evidence, conventional wisdom would suggest that vocabulary instruction would be a prominent aspect of literacy instruction. Unfortunately, a review of American classrooms indicates that has not been the case.

Durkin's classic 1979 observational study revealed that teachers devoted only 19 minutes to vocabulary within a total 4,469 minutes of reading. Roser and Juel (1982) corroborated this instructional deficit, finding that within an individual reading lesson, teachers allocated a meager 5% of their time to vocabulary—an average of only 1.67 minutes per lesson. In 2002, Beck, McKeown, and Kucan encapsulated their concerns in a single statement—"all the available evidence indicates that there is little emphasis on the acquisition of vocabulary in school curricula" (p. 15).

You can reverse this lack of attention to vocabulary by integrating it into your literacy block within protected times. In this model, vocabulary receives 10 minutes of direct instruction each day during whole group as well as dedicated time in guided reading and small-group work—raising the percentage of time devoted to instruction to over 30%!

Students may be studying high-frequency words, words taken from texts they are currently reading (from a guided reading book, an anthology, or a book group selection for more mature students), grade-level word lists, above-level words . . . or a combination of these choices. This is a significant departure from most literacy block models that either don't emphasize vocabulary instruction or do so with an imposed list of words that all students must master regardless of their individual vocabulary skill sets. In the Core Block, you develop a personal word list for your students that targets their unique word learning needs.

While this may seem like an overwhelming task, it is important to remember that the vast majority of today's teachers assign weekly vocabulary lists, and nearly all of them (95%) report adapting them for struggling students. Unfortunately, the most common modification is to assign struggling students fewer words; only 28% of teachers report providing easier words to address their developmental needs (Johnston, 2001). The practice of a reduced word list will certainly produce less frustration in the present—but will also ensure that your struggling students never catch up with their classmates. Your students need a personalized plan for vocabulary instruction—not less words.

How is a personalized word list developed? Integrate vocabulary into two instructional layers—whole-group grade-level vocabulary study and small-group customized vocabulary study. First, to maintain the integrity of literacy instruction and to safeguard against an ever-widening vocabulary gap, your students share a central set of words expected of their class that keeps everyone "on track." Second, along with these focus words, they work in prescriptive vocabulary groups with selected words to address their current vocabulary needs, ensuring that they are receiving targeted instruction as well as collaborative support from other classmates with similar needs. This does not mean that the word list grows. Instead, you create a hybrid list of words that has the power to reduce the vocabulary gap and support individual students in their literacy development. (Personalized word lists will be discussed at length in Chapter 4.)

Let's look inside a classroom where the teacher uses personalized word lists to support her students' vocabulary development. Ms. Jackson is a fifth-grade teacher whose classroom is marked by a wide disparity in vocabulary knowledge. Everyone in her class studies five grade-level appropriate words of high utility from which all students will benefit. In addition, she has one group containing second-language learners who study five high-frequency words (e.g., *fly, again, may, some*, and *once*). Meanwhile, another of her groups comprises struggling readers. They study the same five grade-level words along with five below-level words from a previous grade not yet mastered (e.g., *awkward, peculiar, surface, vacant*, and *jagged*). Other students in her classroom may work collaboratively on five additional words from their grade level or from a text they are reading. A final group of her students have advanced language skills and study five additional words designed to accelerate their vocabulary growth (e.g., *prominent, boisterous, hoax, commentary*, and *inevitable*). In this configuration, Ms. Jackson's students learn the essential words of their current grade-level goals, while shoring up words currently not in their reserves.

Ms. Jackson bases her instructional decisions on the needs of her students, but regardless of the contents of the list, she expects her students to demonstrate their mastery of targeted vocabulary terms by recognizing and understanding the meaning of the selected words, spelling the words correctly, and using them in their daily lives—both in oral and written language. To ensure this level of vocabulary proficiency, she provides ongoing instructional support. This is critical as research indicates that learners require multiple interactions with a vocabulary word before it is mastered (Graves et al., 2014; Hirsch, 2003; Nagy & Scott, 2000; Rupley, 2005; Stahl, 2004). Students need at least 12 exposures before they transition from short-term surface understanding to retaining the word and using it in meaningful contexts (McKeown, Beck, Omanson & Pople, 1985; Nagy, 2005).

Recognizing the level of support and interaction demanded to internalize vocabulary knowledge, you need to ensure students have multiple experiences to utilize words in both oral and written language. In a traditional literacy block, this simply does not happen. The word list is assigned and students are expected to learn them with little instructional attention. (Chapter 4 will provide instructional practices and tasks to ensure that your students are actively engaged with vocabulary acquisition in meaningful, rigorous ways during whole-group instruction, guided reading, and small-group application.)

Comprehension and Fluency. Despite a plethora of research supporting the importance of equipping students with comprehension strategies (National Reading Panel, 2000; Torgesen, 2004), explicit teaching of comprehension strategies is not always fully incorporated in the literacy block, especially for K–2 students. Stahl (2004) makes the argument that "the research demonstrates that instruction in phonological awareness and decoding are not enough if we want students to be able to read and make sense of multiple genres for multiple purposes" (p. 605).

Just as Durkin's 1979 classic teacher observation study revealed insights into vocabulary instruction, she also delved into what happens in classrooms with comprehension instruction. She found that teachers typically used questions from basals and worksheets and focused heavily on story questions. The problem is asking questions about a text already read is not teaching comprehension; it is assessing comprehension. Unfortunately, contemporary researchers continue to report little evidence of daily comprehension instruction (Pressley, 2006; Pressley, Wharton-McDonald, Mistretta, & Echevarria, 1998).

If strategy instruction is in place, however, a different but equally serious concern is how we as teachers present it and how our students come to view it. Too often, the strategy becomes the end point of instruction. Students learn strategies without fully grasping that they function only as tools that readers utilize to make meaning from text. To counter these negative influences, provide explicit strategy instruction during whole group and then embed those strategies in guided reading and small-group application. (Guidelines and specific comprehension strategies will be discussed at more length in Chapter 5.)

Fluency also plays a significant role in students' literacy development (National Reading Panel, 2000; Rasinski, 2004; Samuels, 2012). Commonly characterized as the ability to read with accuracy, automaticity, and prosody, fluency forms the link between word identification and comprehension. Students who struggle with fluency typically direct the majority of their cognitive resources to word identification, leaving little in their reserves to construct meaning.

How can you address fluency with your students? Offer a range of instructional activities designed to improve reading fluency, such as echo reading, choral reading, Readers Theater, rereading, phrasing practice, etc. Chapter 5 will provide a framework for explicit fluency instruction. The key, however, is that your whole-group teaching of fluency skills will be supported in guided reading time as well as during small-group application.

Guided Reading

Guiding reading is universally recognized as an essential component of any literacy block model (Cunningham, Hall, & Cunningham, 2000; Fountas & Pinnell, 1996). Its greatest strength is that it offers you the opportunity, typically the only opportunity within the entire instructional day, to meet with your students in small groups and provide prescriptive support. We believe that until you see the "whites of their eyes" and work with them one-on-one in a small group of students with similar strengths and needs, it can be very difficult to assess what students truly know and what they need. So, guided reading becomes the most important part of your literacy block.

Often, however, guided reading instruction falters in its potential to personalize instruction. Sometimes it is weakened by the frequency teachers meet with guided reading groups. Many literacy block models recommend seeing struggling students every day, on-level students two or three times a week, and above-level students once a week. Does this configuration address the needs of a diverse classroom and ensure equity? Yes, your struggling students receive additional attention, but what happens to your on-level and above-level students? Often their literacy development stagnates. They may not be in academic danger, but neither are they flourishing (Feldhusen, 1992).

Consider the case of high-achieving students who commonly meet the least during guided reading. As the first national report on giftedness, the 1972 Marland Report revealed that gifted students who did not receive appropriate educational experiences functioned at two to four grade levels below their potential. A 1993 federal report echoed these findings describing a "quiet crisis" and asserting that "despite sporadic attention over the years to the needs of bright students, most of them continue to spend time in school working well below their capabilities. . . . They are underchallenged and therefore underachieve" (U.S. Department of Education, 1993, p. 5). Of marked interest are the results of a contemporary study following the achievement of 120,000 high-achieving students, finding that 44% of students identified as "high flyers" dropped from the top tier between third and eighth grade (Xiang et al., 2011).

Another weak spot is the instructional content of the guided reading session. Sometimes, guided reading is linked to the whole-group instruction. Often, it isn't. Thus, a gap forms within the literacy block itself as students focus their attention on one learning objective during whole-group activities and another in guided reading.

Even when linked, however, the guided reading instruction may sometimes be generic. So that although groups have a range of ability levels, the instruction may be nonspecific and non-responsive to individual needs—instead maintaining the same learning objective for all students. This is often the case for commercial programs with teacher scripts.

What are the implications of these weaknesses for effective instruction? The paradigm of guided reading must change. You should meet with all of your guided reading groups every day with prescriptive instruction appropriate to the needs of individual groups linked to whole-group instruction and core instructional goals. We will say it again. You should see every student every day, and yes, the time allotted for each group will decrease. That may appear to be detrimental to learning, but students will actually receive increased direct, explicit instruction. For example, as illustrated in Table 2.2, guided reading groups typically meet for 20 minutes, but with the exception of the lowest-performing group, students only work with the teacher twice a week—or even once a week. With this model, the majority of students receive 40 minutes a week of personalized learning with the teacher, but some as little as 20 minutes.

On the other hand, if you meet all of your groups for 15 minutes daily, every student in your classroom receives 75 minutes a week of prescriptive instruction—nearly double that of the traditional literacy block model (see Table 2.3).

The initial response to this instructional shift is the concern about how productive students can be in a limited time frame as well as how much movement and disturbance will be created

TABLE 2.2 Typical Guided Reading Schedule

Monday	Tuesday	Wednesday	Thursday	Friday
Low	Low	Low	Low	Low
Medium I	Medium II	Medium I	Medium II	High

26 ◆ Foundations of Literacy Instruction

TABLE 2.3 Guided Reading Schedule for the Core Block

Monday	Tuesday	Wednesday	Thursday	Friday
Low	Low	Low	Low	Low
Medium I	Medium I	Medium I	Medium I	Medium I
Medium II	Medium II	Medium II	Medium II	Medium II
High	High	High	High	High

by having students move every 15 minutes. With instructional routines in place, your students should know where they are to be and move quickly with little disruption. Once in their guided reading groups, your instruction should be focused with set procedures so that students have a clear understanding of their responsibilities and you have the ability to monitor their learning daily.

The content of guided reading should also be modified slightly, in this case, to take advantage of the gradual release of responsibility model. The three instructional goals of whole-group instruction are reinforced during guided reading. During the first 2 minutes of each session, review personalized vocabulary with your students. Although brief, this increases the number of interactions students have with words and, consequently, improves the likelihood that students will retain these words in long-term memory and be capable of utilizing them independently. Then, you move into reading a text with the students. Here again the parameters change. Call student attention to word study elements discussed during whole group, such as a focus on r-controlled vowels or a target prefix, that naturally appear in the reading. In addition, rather than asking questions to assess comprehension, encourage your students to practice using the strategies they were introduced to during whole group, as research has demonstrated that strategies should be taught to students as they are engaged in reading—not as a separate activity (Block et al., 2002). This also allows you to use their performance in this setting to identify instructional moves for the whole group. (Chapters 3 through 6 will recommend instructional tasks for guided reading.)

Small-Group Application

As with guided reading, small-group learning activities (e.g., learning centers, learning stations, literacy stations) are commonplace in literacy block models:

> Because students spend a significant amount of time away from the teacher during guided reading, the time question is critical. Clearly, the power of the instruction that takes place away from the teacher must rival the power of the instruction that takes place with the teacher." (Ford & Opitz, 2002, p. 710)

The reality, though, is learning centers change periodically and may or may not correlate to other aspects of literacy instruction. To benefit from the strength of the GRR model as well as to form a consistent link of instruction, connect your small-group application back to your whole-group instruction and guided reading. For a 90-minute literacy block, then, 30 minutes would be devoted to whole-group instruction with the remaining 60 minutes left to guided reading and small-group application. Table 2.4 demonstrates the schedule.

Consider that by adhering to core instruction, your students will interact with the same instructional goals (i.e., word study, vocabulary, and comprehension & fluency) during whole group with the class collectively, again during guided reading in a more collaborative approach, and finally within small-group application activities with an expectation of independent practice.

TABLE 2.4 Core Block Rotation Schedule

	Rotation 1 15 minutes	Rotation 2 15 minutes	Rotation 3 15 minutes	Rotation 4 15 minutes
Guided Reading	A Group	C Group	B Group	D Group
Word Study Center	B Group	D Group	A Group	C Group
Vocabulary Center	C Group	B Group	D Group	A Group
Comprehension & Fluency Center	D Group	A Group	C Group	B Group

Equally important is how the application tasks are utilized. Students should bring their small-group application work with them for whole group the following day and share with the class. Thus, rather than scanning student work on a weekly basis, you can monitor student learning every day. This practice also, once again, adds to the interactions your students have with the content as well as increases their accountability and responsibility for learning.

Thus, small-group application activities complete the chain of core instruction. In effect, whole-group instruction, guided reading, and small-group application form a learning cycle that continues day by day, deepening student learning and gradually releasing responsibility until your students have mastered the core content.

The Core Block "In Action"

Mr. Diaz's second-grade class is learning about hard and soft cs. To introduce the concept, he wrote several examples of words containing the hard *c* sound and several examples of words containing the soft *c* sound. He also taught his students the rule that if the *c* is followed by *a*, *o*, or *u*, the *c* would make a hard sound like a *k*. If, on the other hand, *e*, *i*, or *y* precedes the *c*, the sound will be soft like an *s*. The class practiced the rule with several words. When each group met him in guided reading, he had already identified several examples of these words in their text. Each time such a word appeared, he drew their attention to it and asked them to pronounce it. Then, he asked them to explain what rule they followed to pronounce it correctly. When students went to the Word Study Center, they found a short list of words containing hard and soft *c* sounds. They practiced pronouncing them with a partner and then wrote the word down with an accompanying picture to demonstrate their understanding of it. During their next whole-group time the following day, Mr. Diaz called on students to read the words and share their illustrations. He continued to reinforce their understanding of the rule in guided reading and small-group application time.

Each day during whole-group instruction, he reviewed the work from the previous day and included additional activities to deepen their learning.

The students are also learning a set of core vocabulary words—one of which is *sleep*. Mr. Diaz introduced them to the word during whole group. He wrote it on the board, pronounced it, asked the class to pronounce it, used it in a sentence, and talked to students about when they sleep, how long they sleep, etc. When they met him in their guided reading lesson, he used the first 2 minutes to review personalized vocabulary words. When students moved to small-group application activities and came to the Vocabulary Center, they were instructed to draw a picture of each of their vocabulary words. The next day, everyone brought their illustrations, and Mr. Diaz asked them to show their illustration for each word first to a partner, and then he called on several students to hold up their illustrations for everyone to see and explain how their picture demonstrated the word. The class talked about how the illustrations were the same and how they were different and why they drew what they did. He completed the same activity for 2 to 3 minutes at the beginning of each of his guided reading groups, focusing on their personalized word lists. This allowed his students to engage with their vocabulary words multiple times in varying contexts and learning modes as well as to give him an opportunity to monitor his students' understanding of vocabulary.

In comprehension, Mr. Diaz's class is learning how to identify the lesson, or moral, of a story. During whole group he led a class discussion on the rules that students have in their homes (e.g., do their homework, clean their room), in school (e.g., don't run in the hallway, raise your hand in class before calling out), and in life (e.g., look both ways before crossing the street). Then, he asked his students how these rules came to be and why they exist. He emphasized that people learn lessons in life (e.g., don't run in the hallway) and that we learn lessons every day. Then, he explained that lessons also occur in the work of authors. Authors tell stories that share lessons from life. Reminding students of a story previously read by the class, the students worked collectively to determine what lesson they learned from reading that text. When they came to guided reading, Mr. Diaz asked the group what lesson they were learning from their book, instructing them to refer back to the text to explain their thinking. During small-group application, the students were given a fable and asked what lesson the characters learned. Bringing their written response with them to the next day's whole-group time, students shared their answers with feedback from Mr. Diaz. Then, he devoted the rest of the time teaching them a strategy for determining a story's lesson that they would use during guided reading and small-group application work.

Mr. Diaz has modified his literacy block to focus on core knowledge. Every component of the block works in tandem to strengthen student learning, and by using whole-group time for students to share their work from small-group application he is instilling accountability as well as ensuring daily assessment of their progress.

Conclusion

The Core Block re-envisions the literacy block for the 21st century. It is built on the foundation of the gradual release of responsibility model to provide a framework for instructional practice and to strengthen student learning. Effective teaching and learning in the Core Block also revolve around the balanced literacy components of phonemic awareness, phonics, vocabulary, comprehension, and fluency within whole-group instruction, guided reading, and small-group application . . . as a mosaic of component pieces that fit together to create not just highly effective instruction but also competent, independent readers and writers.

Part II

Components of the Core Block

- ♦ Word Study
- ♦ Vocabulary Development
- ♦ Strategic Reading Instruction
- ♦ Writers' Craft
- ♦ Expanded Reading Opportunities

3

Word Study

Students acquire literacy skills through a developmental process. Miss a step, and students falter. Nowhere in literacy is this truer than in word study. With thousands of words in the English language, it is simply not possible for students to memorize all of the words that they will encounter in text. To develop the necessary word identification strategies, students need to discover how to elicit meaning effectively and efficiently. Word study supports students in this process as it fosters students' knowledge of words and encourages them to explore language as they discover the inherent patterns in words, facilitating both their reading and their spelling.

Its foundation rests on the understanding that English orthography, or spelling, forms three distinct, yet interlocking, layers. Bear and colleagues (2014) identify these layers as Alphabet, Pattern, and Meaning (See Figure 3.1). Each one builds off of the other. First, students must develop alphabetic understanding. They then use that knowledge to cultivate an understanding of pronunciation based on letter patterns, and that information goes on to shape their ability to find meaning in groups of letters like

> "For students of all ages and languages, knowledge of the ways in which their written language represents the language they speak is the key to literacy."
>
> *(Bear et al., 2014, p. 9)*

prefixes, root words, and suffixes. Taken together, word study forms the groundwork of literacy acquisition and development. Nothing else can progress—reading, spelling, or writing—without these first building blocks of language.

The **alphabetic layer** emphasizes phonemic awareness and deepening students' consciousness of the speech sound system and the alphabetic principle. Within this layer, then, phonemic awareness centers on auditory skills and is defined as the ability to hear, identify, and manipulate sounds in spoken words (Reading & Van Deuren, 2007), such as in the example of the word *mat*, which has three phonemes—/m/ /a/ /t/. Meanwhile, the alphabetic principle accentuates the one-to-one correspondence between letters and sounds. Typically taught together, they play a significant causal role in reading acquisition.

This alphabetic layer is a precursor and building block for the **phonics layer,** at which juncture students advance toward identifying patterns of letters and how to use these patterns to read and spell. For example, *dog* follows a pattern of consonant-vowel-consonant (CVC), which indicates that the vowel sound will be short. Students who have learned the CVC pattern have acquired

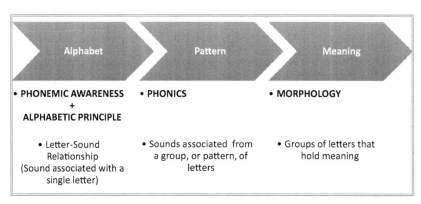

FIGURE 3.1 Developmental Continuum of Word Study

the "code" to sound out words containing that pattern correctly. By consequence, if students recognize the CVC pattern in reading, they will be more likely to use that same knowledge in their spelling of words. Thus, when students attempt to spell the word *mop*, they should hear three distinct sounds with a medial short *o* sound that points them to identify the CVC pattern in the aural word, allowing them to spell *m . . . o . . . p*. Thus, gaining phonics skills supports the inverse yet complementary competencies of word identification (decoding) and spelling (encoding).

The **meaning layer** takes place when students recognize that certain letter groupings contain meaning, such as in prefixes, roots, and suffixes. (Example: The suffix *-ful* in *joyful* is pronounced like the word *full* and indicates "full of joy." The reader also knows that words ending in *-ful* are adjectives so if he or she encounters an unfamiliar word, there is additional syntactical support with determining its meaning.) It is important to note that while these layers are developmental, mature readers utilize all three of them simultaneously when reading and writing.

"A child's level of phonemic awareness on entering school is widely held to be the strongest single determinant of the success that she or he will experience in learning to read – or conversely, the likelihood that she or he will fail."

(Adams, Foorman, Lundberg, & Beeler, 1998, p. 2)

Significance of Word Study for Literacy Achievement

Simply put, students cannot comprehend without first gaining skills at the word identification level. Numerous studies have demonstrated the essential nature of word study in children's literacy development and its effects on reading achievement (Bear, Invernizzi, Templeton, & Johnson, 1996; Bloodgood & Pacifici, 2004; Kirk & Gillon, 2009).

For example, research has conclusively established a link between phonemic awareness skills and reading acquisition (Adams, 1990; Hogan, Catts, & Little, 2005; Mody, 2003; National Reading Council, 1998; National Reading Panel, 2000; Torgesen, 2002), and it continues to be viewed as a powerful predictor of reading achievement—even over IQ (Lyon, 1995; Stanovich, 1994). Thus, students who enter first grade with poor phonemic awareness skills are very likely to remain poor readers in the fourth grade as this gap slows their acquisition of word identification skills (Juel, 1988). The presence, or absence, of this skill set in kindergarten can even predict literacy achievement for those same children 11 years later as high school students (MacDonald & Cornwall, 1995).

Appreciating its influence is crucial, for while many students enter kindergarten with a wealth of oral language, they may not have corresponding skills in phonemic awareness. This can have serious consequences for young children because without planned, explicit instruction, many will fail to acquire it on their own. Students with weak phonemic awareness skills, however, improve quickly with relatively brief sessions of daily explicit instruction (Yopp & Yopp, 2000) with the total number of hours needed for the requisite understanding of phonemic awareness approximating no more than 20 hours.

While phonemic awareness provides an indisputable foundation for literacy acquisition, phonics takes emerging readers to the next level of word identification skills as it transitions into decoding and encoding written language. A code refers to the system that supports understanding of written messages as well as the ability to send them to others—in effect, it creates the capacity to communicate. Phonics opens that "code" to emerging readers, allowing them to understand text written by others as well as to create their own text and communicate with those around them.

A compelling research base comprising prominent large-scale studies also exists that substantiates the power of explicit phonics instruction in reading achievement (Adams, 1990; Anderson, Hiebert, Scott, & Wilkinson, 1985; Chall, 1967; Snow, Burns, & Griffin, 1998). In 2000, The National Reading Panel echoed these findings, recommending that "explicit, systematic phonics instruction is valuable and an essential part of a successful classroom reading program" (p. 10).

As students mature and delve deeper into layers of word study, there is a shift in the need for phonemic awareness, phonics, and morphology—with an increasing need for

"Collectively, studies suggest, with impressive consistency, that programs including systematic instruction on letter-sound correspondences lead to higher achievement in both word recognition and spelling, at least in the early grades and especially for slower or economically disadvantaged students."

(Adams, 1990, p. 32)

morphological awareness and a decreasing need for phonemic awareness (Bowers & Kirby, 2010). Primary texts, for example, contain few morphologically complex words so that in second grade it constitutes only 15% of the variance in vocabulary (McBride-Chang, Wagner, Muse, Chow, & Shu, 2005). By third grade, the number grows to 41%, and by fifth grade it reaches 53% (Carlisle, 2003). As would be expected, then, by fifth grade morphological awareness has greater predictive abilities than phonemic awareness to forecast reading achievement (Mann & Singson, 2003) with morphological awareness accounting for approximately 40% of the variance in reading achievement in Grades 4–9 (Nagy et al., 2006). As with the previous two layers of word study, research has steadfastly identified a correlation among morphology and word identification, spelling, vocabulary acquisition, and reading comprehension (Berninger, Abbott, Nagy, & Carlisle, 2009; Bowers & Kirby, 2010; Carlisle, 2003; Kirby et al., 2012; Kuo & Anderson, 2006; Pacheco & Goodwin, 2013; Tong, Deacon, Kirby, Cain, & Parrila, 2011). Focusing on morphology has proven particularly beneficial for a number of student populations, including younger students, struggling readers, and English language learners, as they use this knowledge to facilitate word identification, spelling, and reading comprehension (Bowers & Kirby, 2010; Carlisle, Stone, & Katz, 2001; Carlo et al., 2004; Casalis, Colé, & Sopo, 2004; Kieffer & Lesaux, 2008; Kim, 2013).

What exactly is morphology? It is the study of morphemes—the smallest units of meaning-bearing language. They include prefixes, roots, and suffixes. When that knowledge is applied as a word identification strategy, it allows readers to generate thousands and thousands of words (Templeton, 2011/2012). Without it, student ability to identify unfamiliar words, infer their meanings, or comprehend text can be severely hindered, which is regularly documented in struggling readers in middle school, high school, and even at the university level (Mahoney, 1994).

A seminal study by Nagy and Anderson in 1984 determined that approximately 60% of words in Grades 3–9 can be inferred through their morphemes and context clues and that students can leverage morphological understanding to "problem solve" three extra words for every new word they learn. As significant as this expertise may be, its value increases even further within the academic disciplines (e.g., science, social studies, math) when that number leaps to over 90% (Green, 2008)! With this potential to increase word identification skills, it is easy to see why morphology should be an essential component of the literacy block.

"Knowledge of 20 prefixes and 14 roots, and knowing how to use them, can unlock up to 100,000 words."

(Gruber, 1986)

Recognizing the potential of word study to enrich student literacy and provide a crucial link between word identification and comprehension, the next step is to ensure that instructional practices in the literacy block reflect an awareness of these layers of English orthography and convert this knowledge into more effective word identification strategies for students. The next section will highlight each of the three layers as we recommend how to implement them within the mini-lessons taught during whole-group instruction as well as during small-group applications, or APP, centers. Let's begin with phonemic awareness.

Phonemic Awareness

Phonemic awareness develops gradually—not all at once. When planning for instruction, consider the larger umbrella of phonological awareness, which includes not just single phonemes but also larger units, such as words and syllables (See Figure 3.2). Students

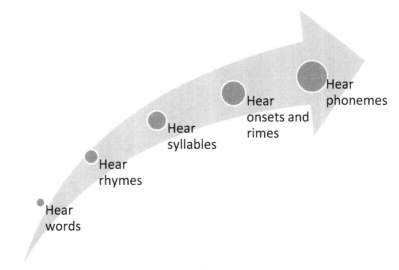

FIGURE 3.2 Phonological Awareness Sequence of Instruction

need to progress sequentially through activities focusing on rhyming, syllables, onset, and rime before coming to phonemes (Yopp & Yopp, 2000).

Within the Core Literacy Block, include both phonemic awareness and alphabetic activities during whole-group instruction and guided reading, with alphabetic activities highlighted during the Word Study APP center. This will allow students to work directly with you to identify sounds and letters, while continuing their acquisition of letter recognition during their small-group time.

Some common alphabet activities include the use of manipulatives (magnetic letters, felt letters, sand box, etc.), alphabet books, alphabet collages, and sorting activities. In the midst of these hands-on experiences, however, don't forget that students need to write—even at this emerging literacy stage—to encourage the cognitive link between sounds and letters. Although many commercial programs emphasize tracing activities, we recommend that students write their own letters. The importance of this was demonstrated in a 2012 study conducted by psychology professor, Karin James, in which she asked pre-literate students to produce a letter in one of three ways: trace the letter from a dotted outline, write the letter in their own handwriting, or type the letter on a computer keyboard. They were then shown the letter again and given a brain imaging scan. The scan showed that students who wrote the letter freehanded had substantial activity in the part of the brain used by adults when they read and write. Those students who traced the letter or used the keyboard showed almost no activity in that part of the brain. James asserted that these results indicate that the physical efforts of handwriting engage the brain's motor pathway, increasing learning gains and correlating to letter identification skills.

At this developing level of literacy acquisition, the feedback loop is less pronounced. Students work in their centers, but they do not have to bring any tangible work with them to the next day's whole-group instruction. You can, however, review the concept practiced in the center to determine how well they are progressing or to determine if you need to provide additional support.

Phonics Development

Phonics instruction should follow a logical sequence that provides opportunities for a gradual release of responsibility—transitioning from teacher modeling, guided practice, and application for learning. It will, as do the other components of word study, require daily mini-lessons during whole-group instruction. The lessons should be focused on the phonics pattern being studied and provide extensive practice with word building and authentic contexts. The patterns that students learn from their phonics study should also guide their spelling so that they can sound out the words that they wish to write—shifting back and forth between decoding others' text to encoding their own words. In fact, this facet of instruction is critical. As inverse cognitive processes, students should decode (read) and encode (spell) every day. Encouraging students to spell words, while reminding them of the inherent phonics patterns, strengthens their retention and application in both word identification and spelling. (Look at Appendix B for the phonics patterns students should master correlated to grade-level benchmarks.)

42 ◆ Components of the Core Block

As you begin to plan for phonics instruction, ensure that whole-group instruction explicitly defines the phonics pattern with numerous real word examples, while the Word Study APP center encourages students to engage with the pattern actively, collaboratively, and with increasingly greater depth of understanding. Meanwhile, when you see students in guided reading, briefly remind them of the target phonics pattern and prompt them to be mindful of this new learning while they are reading. If you notice students struggling with a word that illustrates the phonics pattern, remind them to use this rule in reading text. Lastly, don't forget the strength of the feedback loop. Students should bring their work from the APP center to you the next day during whole group. This allows you to monitor student work and adjust instruction, while your students benefit from multiple, daily exposures of your targeted phonics pattern.

How does the APP center schedule work? Figure 3.3 provides a sample, but let's take a closer look. On Day 1, after you have provided explicit instruction on a targeted phonics pattern, students go the Phonics APP center and complete the first activity in which they read a list of words that highlight the phonics pattern and then sketch an illustration of each word in the list in their reading notebook. While this is a seemingly simple activity and one which students enjoy, it also encourages students to develop mental images of words, providing a concrete representation on which they "hang" new learning. Also, don't forget to have the students write the word as well. It strengthens the physical connection between verbal and nonverbal learning.

During Day 2, when students come to whole-group instruction, they bring their sketches with them. The mini-lesson allows students to review the words they read the previous day and share their illustrations. As you walk about the room and observe students as they share their work with classmates, you can quickly determine if students read the words correctly and understood their meanings—that provides an immediate feedback loop. You may also wish students to share their illustrations with the whole class. Later, they move to the Phonics APP center and complete the second activity, completing a "word hunt" to search for words containing the phonics pattern. Again, this is an outwardly simple task; yet, it encourages students to read text purposefully looking for the phonics pattern in authentic text as well as expanding their learning to identify that phonics pattern in new and unfamiliar words. It also promotes a bit of an informal competition as students race to find as many words as possible before the end of that center.

On Day 3, students will bring these words with them to share. You may ask students to read their words aloud as you write them on the board or invite representatives from each small group to write their lists on the board for everyone to see. In either case, take this time to listen to students reading the words and to check that the words they selected truly do adhere to the phonics pattern. This is a golden opportunity to ensure that students recognize the pattern and are reading words correctly by applying the pattern to real text. If there are errors, now is the time to resolve them—before misunderstandings fester in student thinking. Transitioning later to the Phonics APP center, students complete the third activity, Build-a-Word, in which they read words containing the phonics pattern, use manipulatives to spell these words, and then write them in their reading notebook. This hands-on task promotes kinesthetic learning and word play.

Students on Day 4 bring the list of words they spelled in their reading notebooks and read the words with the class. You may want them to spell the words for a second time during whole group. Once again, the feedback loop allows you to have immediate evidence of their learning and the opportunity to modify your instruction to strengthen student learning. It also increases the accountability of students' independent work. Moving to this day's Phonics APP center, they complete a Phonics Roundup, brainstorming as many words as possible that illustrate the phonics pattern. This typically becomes "game day" as students boast about the number of words they created.

During Day 5 students share their list of generated words during whole-group instruction. It is not uncommon to have lists of 20–30 words. The record number we have seen is 63! If students can create that many words illustrating a targeted phonics pattern, then they truly understand that generalization in the English language. Their last Phonics APP center will build on that word-level knowledge as they craft complete sentences using words that share the target phonics pattern, ensuring that phonics development is not relegated to skills in isolation but rather to utilizing this knowledge meaningfully, authentically, and purposefully.

Day 1: Picture Words. Teacher delivers explicit instruction on phonics pattern with accompanying words that illustrate the generalization. Then, students go to the center and read a list of 5–10 words (already taught—or for more challenging work—new words that adhere to the pattern) that are concrete, visual terms. The students write each word down in their notebooks, read the word, and then draw a picture of the word they read.

Day 2: Word Hunt. Students use a current text (anthology, guided reading book, independent reading book, newspaper, content area text, etc.) to "search" for words containing the phonics pattern being studied. Once "found," they write the words in their notebook. Each student should find 5–10 words (at your discretion).

Day 3: Build-a-Word. Teacher places a sheet of paper with the phonics pattern listed and 3–5 examples of real words illustrating that pattern. Students use manipulatives (foam letters, letter stamps, magnetic letters, letter cards, letter tiles, etc.) to "build" words adhering to that pattern. After they construct the words with manipulatives, they also write down the new words in their notebook.

Day 4: Phonics Roundup. Students brainstorm as many words as they can that adhere to the target phonics pattern. The group with the most correct words is the winner!

Day 5: Words in Action. Teacher places a sheet of paper with 5–10 words highlighting the target phonics pattern. Students must write one sentence for each word, spelling the word correctly as well as following syntactic rules.

FIGURE 3.3 Phonics APP Center

While other phonics activities can be used during this time, the ones highlighted in Figure 3.3 are associated with research-based practices that support emerging readers and boost student achievement. For example, none of the activities include worksheets. Despite the prevalence of worksheets—especially in commercial reading programs—research has consistently revealed no benefit to the completion of worksheets (Anderson et al., 1985; Fisher & Hiebert, 1990; Lipson, Mosenthal, Mekkelsen, & Russ, 2004). In contrast, the APP center work necessitates students be actively involved, exploring language through hands-on, authentic experiences while working under your direction and support.

Morphology

Before moving to instructional practices for morphology, let's consider how morphemes help readers grasp word meanings. A morpheme itself can be defined as a word or word chunk that bears meaning. For example, *tree* is one morpheme. It cannot be broken down and still retain meaning. As this morpheme is a word that can stand alone, it is called a **free morpheme**.

If *s* is added to the end of the word, however, we now have a new word with a new meaning. The word, *trees*, now refers to the plural form of the original free morpheme. Thus, *s* is a morpheme, but it does not hold any meaning by itself. The same example is true with *-ly*. This suffix is a word chunk that holds meaning but only in conjunction with a whole word. These types of morphemes that hold meaning—but only when affixed to base words—are called **bound morphemes**.

Bound morphemes contain two main types—inflectional morphemes and derivational morphemes. **Inflectional morphemes** are grammatical markers that attach at the end of words, thereby changing the meaning of the words to reflect number, possession, verb tense, or comparison. These morphemes are relatively few, predictable in relation to their effect on words, and typically learned in primary grades. Table 3.1 highlights common examples found in English.

46 ◆ Components of the Core Block

TABLE 3.1 Inflectional Morphemes

Inflectional Morpheme	Attached to Free Morpheme	Function	Examples
-s	Noun	To make a noun plural	The boys are playing.
-es	Noun	To make a noun plural	The boxes are on the floor.
-en	Noun	To make irregular nouns plural	Oxen were used on farms long ago.
-'s	Noun	To make singular noun possessive	The dog's bone is buried.
-s'	Noun	To make plural noun possessive	The girls' dresses are pretty.
-s	Verb	To make verb agree with singular subject	John plays the piano.
-ing	Verb	To use the verb as present progressive	John is playing the piano now.
-ed	Verb	To use the verb in past tense	John played the piano yesterday.
-en	Verb	To use the verb as a past participle	Tara has eaten her dessert already.
-er	Adjective/ Adverb	To show comparison between two adjectives or adverbs	He is taller than his brother.
-est	Adjective/ Adverb	To show comparison between three or more adjectives or adverbs	He is the tallest boy in his class.

A **derivational morpheme** operates differently than an inflectional morpheme in that it not only changes the meaning of the root word but also has the ability to change the grammatical form of the morpheme to which it is affixed. It may attach in front of the word (prefix) or at the end of the word (suffix). Table 3.2 illustrates some examples of derivational morphemes.

As a general guide, grades one and two focus on inflectional endings. At this initial level, you should be able to embed them naturally into your daily instruction. If, however, your students struggle with these simple morphemes, you may find it necessary to shift to morphology intermittently as a Word Study target

TABLE 3.2 Derivational Morphemes

Derivational Morpheme	Type	Location	Meaning	Examples
bi-	prefix	affixed before the base word	two	bicycle biannual
pre-	prefix	affixed before the base word	before, earlier than	preview prehistoric
-ism	suffix	affixed after the base word	to practice or support	patriotism
-ology	suffix	affixed after the base word	the study of something	biology geology

skill for your whole-group mini-lesson as well as the Word Study APP center in order to strengthen student learning in this area. Meanwhile, students in grades three through six will benefit from derivational morphemes with an emphasis on the most common prefixes and suffixes along with frequently used root words. By seventh and eighth grade, the spotlight should shift to less familiar derivational morphemes as well as content-based morphemes. (Appendix C contains a comprehensive list of morphemes aligned to grade levels.)

As with the other Word Study components, target morphemes are introduced in the Word Study mini-lesson offered during whole-group instruction. Depending on the level of morphemic knowledge your students possess, you should focus on between two to three morphemes per instructional unit. After explicit instruction on the meaning of the morphemes, students move to small-group work at the Morphology APP center. Figure 3.4 offers a sample morphology APP center schedule, or you can create your own activities.

Let's take a look at some sample morphology activities. On Day 1, introduce the targeted morphemes, define them in explicit terms, and highlight them in multiple words. Then, when students move to the Morphology APP center, they practice defining new words that contain the target morphemes. While a straightforward activity, it encourages students to notice morphemes in real words and practice breaking apart words into meaningful chunks.

Day 1: Tear-Away Words

Teacher gives students 5–10 words containing targeted morphemes. Students must define the words based on their understanding of the morphemes.

Day 2: Morpheme Match-Up

Teacher writes words containing targeted morphemes on index cards or sentence strips and then cuts the words apart, dividing the targeted morpheme from the remainder of the word. Mixing the words up, students must re-assemble the cards into correct words. Then, they write the words in their notebooks. They may use dictionaries to verify their work.

Day 3: Morpheme Word Knowledge

Teacher gives students a list of words all containing targeted morphemes. Students must classify each word based on its part of speech (e.g., noun, verb, adjective, or adverb), write out an explanation for making that decision, and use the word in a sentence.

Day 4: Morpheme Bonanza

Students are given a list of targeted morphemes and create a list of as many words as possible that contain those morphemes. They may use their dictionaries to verify their work.

Day 5: Alike and Different

Students are given a list of words containing targeted morphemes. They must define the word and then provide a synonym and an antonym of that word.

FIGURE 3.4 Morphology Center

They will share their work during Day 2's whole-group instruction on Word Study. This will allow them to demonstrate their understanding while providing you the opportunity to monitor their learning at the onset. After dissecting morphemes in order to build understanding, the next small-group work task is to link individual morphemes into meaningful wholes. The Morpheme Match-Up activity encourages physical manipulation of morphemes as well as a bit of play as students consider some silly words when attaching different morphemes to one another. The dictionary check at the end of the activity ensures that students finish the activity with real words and meaningful learning.

Again on Day 3, students will bring the words they constructed to whole group and explain why they grouped the morphemes in the way that they did and explain the definition of these newly formed words based on their knowledge of the target morphemes. During center time, they are asked to categorize words containing target morphemes into parts of speech and then use that word in a sentence, demonstrating their grasp of how words change based on the type of morpheme that is added to a word as well as their grasp of how morphemes influence a word's syntax. As simple as this activity may sound, students often do not make the cognitive link that morphemes not only have meaning but also create grammatical changes.

Day 4 necessitates students communicate how they classified the words and their rationale for doing so as well as the sentences they constructed. This is an important lesson. You need to determine if students fully grasp the grammatical context that morphemes establish as well as how to use words containing these morphemes correctly in daily language. Later during center time, they will brainstorm as many words as possible containing target morphemes. They may use a dictionary, notes, or other resources. This tends to become competitive as students strive to generate the largest list.

Students will share their words during Day 5's whole-group instruction. They can also add to their respective lists when they hear words that they did include in their own work. Take the time to question students to the meanings of words not previously discussed and encourage them to identify where they found words. Their last center work requires them to review a list of words containing the target morphemes and determine synonyms and antonyms of that word. While they may use a dictionary and thesaurus, this assignment requires them to understand the words at a deeper level as they construct meaning from word parts.

When working in schools, occasionally a teacher will tell us that students are struggling and just don't seem to be acquiring the target skill. After visiting the classroom, what we usually find is that while the students may work in the APP center there is no feedback loop or just a cursory check of work. For the literacy block to be effective, and by extension for your students to be successful, you need to adhere to the feedback loop every day. Without this accountability measure, students may not complete the APP center activities or may continue to work under a misunderstanding of the skill—and without your diligence in checking their work this error continues in their thinking. Lastly, the feedback loop recognizes the work of students and provides them much-needed social interaction in which they express their own learning, gain from the insight and efforts of their classmates, and reap yet another exposure to the skill. So, while we encourage you to create activities for your own APP centers beyond the samples we have included, make certain that you maintain the feedback loop in order to safeguard your instructional capacity and your students' learning potential.

Word Study "In Action"

Ms. Taylor's sixth-grade class is learning about suffixes. Her target morphemes are -*ify*, -*ous*, and -*some*. During her initial mini-lesson in whole-group instruction, she explained that -*ify* is a suffix that means *to become* and transforms a word that has previously been categorized as a noun into a verb. The examples that she gave her students included *fortify*, *solidify*, and *intensify*. Dissecting the word for her class, she highlighted the base word of each example and explained how the suffix altered the meaning of the words as well as their syntax. For example, solid describes a completely filled up object like an ice cube. An ice cube is a solid. However,

Word Study ◆ 51

before it becomes ice, it is simply water. Water must be at an extremely cold temperature in order to become an ice cube—in order to become a solid. Thus, frozen water "solidifies" into ice. A solid is a noun, but when -*ify* is added as a suffix, the word becomes a verb. Ms. Taylor continued her explanation throughout her Word Study lesson for the suffixes -*ous* and -*some* as well.

The class then used those target morphemes in all of their work at the Morphology APP center in the following days. For example, they dissected a list of words in the Tear-Away Words activity as an excerpt from Figure 3.5 illustrates and then discussed them the following day during whole-group instruction.

The students also completed a Morpheme Match-Up, combining target morphemes and base words together, such as in Figure 3.6. Most students correctly linked the morphemes, but for those who struggled, Ms. Taylor explained the meanings and demonstrated dictionary use as a means to check their work.

They went on to show their Morpheme Word Knowledge by sorting words into parts of speech based on their suffixes. When students came to whole group the following day to share their work, Ms. Taylor emphasized how certain morphemes always produce a specific part of speech (e.g., -*ify* is a suffix and will always form a verb when attached to a base word, like in the word *terrify*), while others may create different parts of speech that will necessitate students looking at the work in context to determine its grammatical form (e.g., *foursome* is a noun; *tiresome* is an adjective). Figure 3.7 offers an example of their work.

Word List	Student Answers
hazardous	hazard + ous = full of hazards (An oil spill is hazardous.)
humorous	humor + ous = full of humor (Clowns are humorous.)
simplify	simpl + ify = to make simple (Computers help us simplify our lives.)
troublesome	trouble + some = characterized by being trouble (My little brother is troublesome.)
awesome	awe + some = characterized or inspiring awe (The Grand Canyon is awesome.)

FIGURE 3.5 Tear Away Words

52 ◆ Components of the Core Block

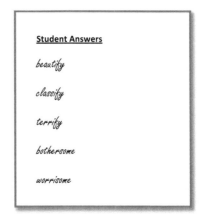

FIGURE 3.6 Morpheme Match-Up

FIGURE 3.7 Morpheme Word Knowledge

During the Morpheme Bonanza, they brainstormed as many words as possible with the target morphemes as shown in Figure 3.8. The students who had the most words were crowned "Vocabulary Kings" and "Vocabulary Queens."

Lastly, Ms. Taylor's class looked at a list of words containing the targeted morphemes. Using knowledge gained from the Morphology APP center and ongoing interaction with suffixes, they defined each word and determined if it had a synonym or an antonym.

Student Brainstorming List

electrify	adventurous	adventuresome
dignify	advantageous	fearsome
satisfy	malicious	handsome
dissatisfy	rebellious	gruesome
identify	glamorous	loathsome
glorify	mountainous	quarrelsome
mystify	delirious	bothersome
magnify	odorous	twosome
citify	grievous	flavorsome
disqualify	murderous	irksome
intensify	dangerous	lonesome
certify	marvelous	
electrify	spacious	
unify	joyous	

FIGURE 3.8 Morpheme Bonanza

Word List

wearisome

electrify

falsify

magnify

spacious

numerous

Student Answers

Word	Definition	Synonym	Antonym
wearisome	to make tired	boring, dull	energetic
electrify	to make electric	excite	bore
falsify	to make false	lie	honest
magnify	to make larger	enlarge	minimize
spacious	to have space	roomy	cramped
numerous	many	a lot, plentiful	few

FIGURE 3.9 Alike and Different

After examining the target morphemes in a number of ways and analyzing how they influence both meaning and part of speech, Ms. Taylor's students feel confident that they understand the suffixes they have been studying, and Ms. Taylor is taking every opportunity within the literacy block as well as in other content area study to encourage their use of morphemes to improve their word identification skills, vocabulary development, and reading comprehension.

Conclusion

Word study should be an essential component of any comprehensive literacy block and a significant focus for daily instruction. Consisting of three layers—phonemic awareness, phonics, and morphology—students transition through these developmentally as they gain knowledge and experience with the English language. Of concern, however, is the need to understand that many students will not cultivate these skill sets without direct, intentional, and continuing attention.

Within the Core Literacy Block, word study becomes a primary focus within whole-group instruction, guided reading, and small-group application centers. If planned carefully, this element of the literacy block offers significant enhancement to students' word identification skills, improving their vocabulary acquisition as well as overall reading comprehension.

4

Vocabulary Development

Vocabulary is a predominant factor in constructing meaning from text, and those who lack a strong vocabulary base will struggle to become independent readers. Vocabulary, then, must be an integral aspect of literacy instruction. It cannot be expected to be acquired solely through incidental reading or as a by-product of a commercial program. Rather, you must make it your priority every day, every class, and for every student.

Significance of Vocabulary for Literacy Achievement

An inarguable link exists between vocabulary knowledge and reading comprehension (Chall, Jacobs, & Baldwin, 1990; Davis, 1944; National Reading Panel, 2000; Stahl & Nagy, 2006) with word meanings comprising between 70% and 80% of reading comprehension (Bromley, 2007). As discussed in Chapter 3, during the early stages of literacy development phonemic awareness is highly predictive of reading achievement, but by fourth grade,

> Vocabulary deficits are the primary cause of academic failure for disadvantaged students in grades 3 through 12.
> *(Becker, 1977)*

vocabulary has become the stronger predictor of reading achievement, and by middle school, vocabulary emerges as the primary prognostic source (Lesaux & Kieffer, 2010).

While primary classrooms commonly emphasize word identification skills, without a corresponding emphasis on developing robust vocabulary, students in the middle elementary grades will demonstrate weaknesses in reading comprehension (Becker, 1977). In fact, even waiting until third grade to begin explicit vocabulary instruction may be too late (Coyne, Capozzoli-Oldham, & Simmons, 2012) as most of the vocabulary gap forms before third grade (Biemiller & Slonim, 2001). The consequence of an over-emphasis of word identification skill building in the absence of focused vocabulary instruction may manifest itself in the creation of students who are "word callers." These are the students who appear to read fluently yet cannot comprehend what they are reading. A recent study found that struggling readers—both native speakers as well as English language learners—typically had sound word reading skills but tended to be word callers (Lesaux & Kieffer, 2010).

This issue was raised by Chall in 1990 when she classified word knowledge into two main categories: word-recognition vocabulary and meaning vocabulary. Word-recognition vocabulary consists of those words students can pronounce, or call out, either through decoding or memorization without being able to identify their meanings. In contrast, meaning vocabulary refers to the ability to define words—an aspect of vocabulary instruction that cannot be lost if students are to make meaning of text and truly comprehend what they are reading. Thus, it is imperative that vocabulary is not viewed as simply calling out words . . . but rather as a conscious understanding of word meanings.

This "meaning" vocabulary has significant bearing on reading comprehension, especially when viewed through the lens of the breadth and depth of students' vocabulary knowledge. While breadth can be characterized by the sheer number of words students have at least a basic understanding, depth refers to the degree of their understanding and encompasses pronunciation, spelling, morphological awareness, meaning, and syntax (Carlo et al., 2004; Qian, 1999). In a quest to ensure students enhance their vocabulary knowledge, many educators emphasize the breadth of word learning that causes them to increase the number of words assigned, thus allotting students too many words to learn, and more importantly, to retain. Conversely, we recommend that you concentrate on vocabulary depth—students must gain vigor to their word learning if they are to "own" these words and incorporate them within their listening vocabulary, speaking vocabulary, reading vocabulary, and written expression.

Another lens through which you might view the breadth and depth of vocabulary is the developmental psychology concept of fast mapping versus extended mapping in word learning. First introduced by Carey and Bartlett in 1978, fast mapping mirrors the incidental learning that students experience when they encounter a word in context. While they may be able to create a basic understanding and retain it in their memory on a short-term basis, only when students engage in sustained study of the word with multiple exposures does extended mapping allow them to transition from a superficial understanding to a deeper level and retain it in a more permanent capacity (Christ & Wang, 2010). This extended mapping, then, becomes a crucial factor of word learning, which is why we channel vocabulary acquisition within the Core Literacy Block through multiple, interactive engagements with words.

Key Principles for Robust Vocabulary Acquisition

Decades of researchers have investigated vocabulary—its development, its effects on literacy development, and the best practices of instruction that support student learning. From this plethora of research, several principles have emerged that suggest the characteristics of an effective vocabulary program.

At the foundation of this discussion remains the ongoing debate in the reading field as to the relative benefits of direct instruction of words versus teaching word learning strategies—such as morphological analysis and context clues. It is impossible to teach all of the words that students will naturally encounter in their reading lives, and many literacy experts believe that students learn more words from incidental reading than direct instruction (Nagy, Anderson, & Herman, 1987); others counter that explicit instruction on target vocabulary words cannot be overlooked. Biemiller (2001), for example, argues that between 50% and 80% of new words can be acquired through direct instruction. Of equal concern is the awareness that struggling readers are less able to utilize context to explain meanings than their more capable counterparts identified as good comprehenders (Cain, Lemmon, & Oakhill, 2004). Recognizing the value of both explicit and incidental word learning, a balanced approach offers students advantages of both philosophies (Kelley, Lesaux, Kieffer, & Faller, 2010). Within the Core Literacy Block model, students are given opportunities for incidental reading (e.g., read alouds, independent reading, book groups, and project based learning) in which they can utilize their word-learning skills (e.g., morphological analysis and context clues). In addition, the vocabulary component of the Core Literacy Block also focuses on direct instruction of target words. Working in tandem, these opposing instructional philosophies elicit the strength of word learning from all facets of vocabulary acquisition and serve to reinforce one another.

For educators who incorporate direct vocabulary instruction, many still rely on commercial programs. While they are easy to use with ready-made materials and student activities, they have not been proven effective (Blachowich, Fisher, Ogle, & Watts-Taffe, 2006). In a study conducted in 2005, Hiebert revealed that the majority of words generated by one particular fourth-grade basal series would rarely be encountered by students in daily reading (less than once in a million words of text). How then should educators select vocabulary? For the most effective use of time and learning potential, words should be chosen based on their level of utility (Beck, McKeown, & Kucan, 2002; Hiebert, 2005). There are numerous ways to approach this task, but Beck, McKeown, and Kucan (2002) organized words into three principal tiers that are simple to navigate and can easily be used to plan instruction. Tier 1 centers on every day, high-frequency words that students should know on sight (e.g., *dog, brown, upon*). Tier 2 includes high-frequency words for "mature" readers that would be seen across contexts and disciplines (e.g., *cease, benevolent, scold*), and Tier 3 comprises content-based words from academic domains (e.g., *peninsula, equation, photosynthesis*). Using these tiers as a guide, you can intentionally identify words that have the greatest capacity to influence students' vocabulary acquisition and, in turn, reading comprehension, without diverting student attention to words with little use in daily reading tasks. In other words, every time you select a word to be included in explicit vocabulary study, ask yourself how many times your students will encounter this word. If it is an interesting or unusual word, like *serendipity*, that would not be found often, then define the word when your students see it in text and move on in the reading. If, however, it is a word that you expect students will see on a recurring basis, like *prohibit*, then include that in your explicit vocabulary study. With so many words students must know, you don't have time to waste . . . select only those words that have high utility.

With vocabulary words selected, an additional principle is that students benefit from explicit instruction (Christ & Wang, 2010; National Reading Panel, 2000) in a variety of contexts (Beck, McKeown, & Kucan, 2002). Even 10–15 minutes of daily explicit instruction can have powerful effects on word learning (Sobolak, 2011), which has been capitalized on in the Core Literacy Block with students receiving 10 minutes of daily explicit instruction followed by 2–3 minutes of teacher-facilitated study in guided reading and 15 minutes of small-group work in the Vocabulary APP center. Taken together, students gain nearly 30 minutes of daily vocabulary instruction daily—over 2 hours a week!

Another practice commonly found in literacy blocks is the assignment of students using dictionaries to look up definitions as a means to learn new vocabulary. Despite its prevalence in classrooms, assigning students to look up words in a dictionary has been consistently found to be detrimental to learning. In addition to the time required for students to find the definitions and write them down, a fundamental obstacle is that students often misinterpret the definitions (Marzano, 2004; Scott & Nagy, 1997). In contrast to this customary practice, teachers should provide child-friendly definitions (Beck & McKeown, 2007) that explain meanings in everyday language and connect these words to students' prior knowledge.

As you begin to plan for vocabulary activities, it is also helpful to remember that for students to learn and retain new words, they should be immersed and actively engaged in word learning rather than passively completing worksheets or answering questions from a workbook. One aspect of active engagement is the use of repetition and multiple exposures of words in a variety of contexts (Christ & Wang, 2010; Coyne, Capozzoli-Oldham, & Simmons, 2012). How many exposures are enough? Researchers haven't reached a consensus, suggesting 6–20 exposures (Vadasy & Nelson, 2012; Zahar, Cobb, & Spada, 2001), but recent literature from the field suggests perhaps at least 12 exposures may be needed if students are to learn a word deeply and retain it in long-term memory (McKeown, Beck, & Sandora, 2012). The Core Block focuses heavily on this principle as vocabulary study is infiltrated throughout the literacy block and concentrated on in the Vocabulary APP center—all of which encompasses daily opportunities for students to interact and manipulate words in a variety of ways.

Another principle in vocabulary instruction that has a strong research base is using word play as a means to develop and encourage students' word consciousness (Blachowicz, Fisher, & Watts-Taffe, 2005; Kelley, Lesaux, Kieffer, & Faller, 2010). This encompasses games, pantomime, drama, word hunts, contests, etc. An engaging example of word play is encouraging students to use their bodies to demonstrate the meaning of a word, such as how one *sneaks* into a room or the look on someone's face who is *infuriated*. Such engagement can produce a better understanding of the word as well as increased retention (Amiryousefi &

Ketabi, 2011). Word play can be found in the Vocabulary APP center when students participate in word hunts, games, and contests.

Lastly, vocabulary acquisition is greatly enhanced by two oft-forgotten components—speaking and writing. While writing has often been described as a means to make thinking visible, the talk that precedes it allows students to clarify their learning so that writing can transform these basic ideas into a cohesive knowledge base and strengthen retention (Rivard & Straw, 2000). Talk is critical to the learning process (Blachowicz & Fisher, 2012; Cazden, John, & Hymes, 1972; Vygotsky, 1934/1962), and students benefit from collaborative activities with structured discussions in which they interact with their peers. Likewise, writing plays a fundamental role in learning. Kelley and colleagues (2010) even make the argument that "if we are going to close the achievement gap and develop students' critical thinking and oral- and written-language skills, we need to provide students with significant opportunities to speak and write" (p. 10). Because of this interdependence of speaking and writing to enhance learning, students should have ongoing opportunities to talk about their understanding of word meanings during whole-group instruction, guided reading, and APP center work as well as time to participate in writing tasks that encourage them to think about words more deeply and in different contexts than typically encountered in most classrooms.

Personalized Vocabulary Study

Teach to the middle. It is a common phrase heard every day. Educators struggle with differentiating instruction to meet the varied needs of diverse students and ultimately feel compelled to address the needs of the majority. With so many different students, how can a teacher possibly provide vocabulary instruction designed for individual students? It can be done— prescriptively, systematically, and efficiently. First, you must change your current mindset. Students don't benefit from identical word lists. Students come to our classrooms with different strengths and weaknesses and with a wide range of vocabulary levels. Why, then, do we persist in teaching them the same words as if they are all alike? Why waste the time of a student who knows most of the words on the "weekly" list already or frustrate the struggling reader who knows none of the words and appears to be overwhelmed with the quantity and complexity of the words being assigned to learn?

Begin by considering the development of personalized word study. The initial step is to identify the vocabulary knowledge that students currently possess. This can be done through a simple vocabulary assessment like the San Diego Quick Assessment (LaPray & Ross, 1969) that provides graded word lists from pre-primer to 11th grade, isolating students' independent (0–1 word missed), instructional (2 words missed), and frustration levels (3 words missed) for vocabulary study. For insight into students' knowledge of high-frequency words, the Fry Instant Sight Word List (Fry, Kress, & Fountoukidis, 2000) or the Dolch List (Buckingham & Dolch, 1936) can be helpful. Using these or other vocabulary placement assessments, pinpoint students' vocabulary knowledge so that you can target instruction for each student.

With vocabulary levels identified, the next decision is to determine how many words students will learn during a given unit. Although different recommendations exist, a general rule is to teach 10–12 words per week (Biemiller, 2004). From this designated number, establish a sub-set of that word list to encompass grade-level appropriate vocabulary that constitutes a core list that all students will study. These are essential words that allow you to maintain fidelity to your grade-level curriculum as well as providing your students the necessary vocabulary to ensure rigorous study. The grade-level words may come from a text students are reading, a commercial program, or a grade-level list. Just ensure that the words that you choose have a high-utility factor.

Then, analyze the data regarding individual students. Which students have vocabulary levels below that of their grade placement? Select words based on their current working knowledge to comprise a second sub-set of the total vocabulary terms to shore up the gap that exists between them and their peers. Likewise, which students have vocabulary levels above that of their grade placement? Don't allow them to stagnate. Choose words for them that are more advanced than the grade-level words for which they are currently placed. For those students with vocabulary knowledge on level, they will benefit from additional words at their current grade placement to sustain their growth.

Personalized word study may sound cumbersome and difficult to sustain. It isn't. The most arduous task will be to assess all of your students. After that is accomplished, you commonly find groups of students who share similar word knowledge levels that will allow them to study the same word list and work together to increase their vocabulary acquisition. What does it look like in the classroom? Core grade-level words that all students study are taught during whole-group instruction. Personalized word lists are taught for the first 2 to 3 minutes of guided reading as vocabulary levels generally influence reading comprehension levels. Thus, those at a comparable reading level will commonly have a similar vocabulary level. During the Vocabulary APP centers, students work with both their core vocabulary list as well as their prescriptive vocabulary list.

What would a personalized word list look like? Although it may be individualized for just one student, prescriptive lists commonly address multiple students' needs. In a typical classroom, there may be a group of students significantly below grade level, a group somewhat below grade level, a group of on-level students, and a group of students who demonstrate vocabulary knowledge above grade level. An example of the word lists for a fifth-grade classroom is in Table 4.1.

With students assessed and personalized word lists prepared, it is time to plan for instruction. Core words should be introduced during whole-group instruction, using student-friendly definitions, real-life examples, and connections made to students' lives. Guided reading sessions provide 2 to 3 minutes daily to discuss prescriptive words. Students then take their unique word lists

64 ◆ Components of the Core Block

TABLE 4.1 Personalized Vocabulary Study for Grade 5 Word Lists

Words	Significantly Below Level	Somewhat Below Level	On Level	Above Level
Core Words That All Students Study				
1	bravery	bravery	bravery	bravery
2	reveal	reveal	reveal	reveal
3	local	local	local	local
4	discrimination	discrimination	discrimination	discrimination
5	crisis	crisis	crisis	crisis
6	persuade	persuade	persuade	persuade
Prescriptive Words for Targeted Students				
7	hopeful	generous	obligated	dictator
8	joy	annoy	mutter	archaic
9	wrap	awkward	amplify	treacherous
10	crawl	brief	fracture	harmony
11	float	maintain	infection	deteriorate
12	caught	seldom	frantic	infinite

and complete hands-on, collaborative activities in the Vocabulary APP center.

Vocabulary APP Centers

In planning center work, it is helpful to view these collaborative activities as designing a scaffolded pathway to vocabulary acquisition, which can be accomplished by transitioning students through three levels of word knowledge—association, comprehension, and generation (Baumann & Kame'enui, 1991). Associative word knowledge refers to students' ability to define a word and link it to a single context. This may be accomplished through visualization activities and student-friendly definition work. Deepening to a comprehension level, students must be able to manipulate the word to identify synonyms and antonyms, classify it into meaningful categories, etc. At the generative level, students must be able to produce the word within an original context, such as using the word correctly within sentence or

Vocabulary Development ◆ 65

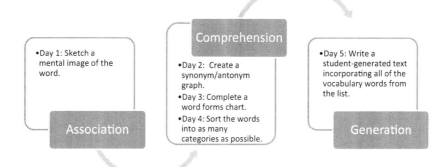

FIGURE 4.1 Vocab APP Center Activities Aligned to Levels of Vocabulary Acquisition

paragraph writing. To facilitate deepening levels of word knowledge, students should actively participate in center work that naturally flows through the three levels, such as in the sample activities illustrated in Figure 4.1.

When focusing on vocabulary acquisition, collaboration remains a key element in learning. Research demonstrates the benefits of students working in small groups while they interact with vocabulary and engage in word learning (Bryant, Goodwin, Bryant, & Higgins, 2003). The feedback loop linking center work and whole-group instruction provides another avenue for students to talk about their word learning activities during center time and then deepen their understanding through social interaction and support by the teacher during whole-group instruction and guided reading.

Let's take a look at each of the sample activities from Figure 4.1. First, Day 1 supports students as they develop "associations" with the words being studied. A simple, but powerful, strategy is to foster word meanings with mental imagery. While vocabulary is often viewed as a completely verbal skill, students learn more deeply and retain that learning longer if given the opportunity to "dual code" information. In Dual Coding Theory, information is retained in permanent memory when it includes both linguistic (language-based) and nonlinguistic (image-based) representations of the word. Looking at multiple studies utilizing nonlinguistic strategies, Powell (1980) reported that this approach produced gains of 34 percentage points in vocabulary learning. In comparing more traditional approaches, nonlinguistic strategies produced a 37-percentage point gain over reviewing definitions and a 21-percentage point gain over just writing student-generated sentences. Based on this research as well as our own instructional experiences, students in Day 1 draw images to reinforce vocabulary knowledge (Blachowicz & Fisher, 2012) such as the sample in Figure 4.2.

FIGURE 4.2 Illustration of the Word "Joy"

During Day 2, students delve into the "comprehension" of the words by creating a synonym/antonym chart. Identifying synonyms and antonyms of target words allows students to expand their understanding of words (Stahl & Nagy, 2006). Synonyms can be particularly effective for helping students to augment their understanding of adjectives and adverbs (Blachowicz, Fisher, & Watts-Taffe, 2005) as well as their ability to retain the word. A study conducted by Boulware-Gooden and colleagues (2007) found that students who generated synonyms and antonyms demonstrated greater increases on vocabulary measures (40%) over that of students who only wrote the vocabulary word and used it in a sentence. Similarly, Powell (1986) argues that incorporating antonym study offers the potential of being one of the most powerful vehicles for vocabulary learning. Table 4.2 illustrates an excerpt from such a chart. This work, however, must be supported by the whole-group instruction that follows it as students grapple with the gradient meanings of these words.

Students may work together to locate synonyms and antonyms and should have access to dictionaries and thesauri (both in print version and online). While this work certainly supports word learning, it is the feedback loop that takes place during the next day's whole-group instruction where the power of this activity shines. For example, a student may have listed happiness as a synonym to joy. The teacher, however, now has the opportunity to clarify that relationship with the class. She or he may pose the following questions: "Is joy exactly the same as happiness?" "Can someone have happiness but not experience joy?" "How would someone look who is joyful?" "What does happiness look like?" "Is there a discernible difference?" "Have you felt joyful?" "Was it the same feeling as happiness?" This type of dialogue encourages students to consider the nuances of words more fully and how uniquely each word may be used within the context of a situation.

TABLE 4.2 Synonym/Antonym Chart

Word	Synonym	Antonym
joy	happiness, bliss	unhappiness, sadness

68 ◆ Components of the Core Block

TABLE 4.3 Word Forms Chart

Word	Noun	Verb	Adjective	Adverb
joy	joy/joyfulness	enjoy	joyful/ enjoyable	joyfully

Day 3 intensifies the learning experience by tasking students to complete a word form chart. A word form chart encourages syntactic exploration to discover if the word has a noun, verb, adjective, or adverb form. This kind of thinking furthers word analysis with prefixes, suffixes, and root words as well as potentially increasing the number of words learned as illustrated in the excerpt in Table 4.3.

The benefit of this activity, then, is not just deepening word knowledge of a single word but multiplying the number of words acquired. In the case of the sample in Table 4.3, the student now has been exposed to not one word—but six words. This focus on parts of speech also supports student awareness of how words are utilized syntactically so that they begin to use words correctly within their speaking and writing. We will caution that this is the most difficult activity in these samples as many students do not have a firm grasp of parts of speech. If you find that your students struggle with this activity, you may want to scaffold their work. Begin with just nouns and verbs. After a couple of weeks or so, add in adjectives. Then, slowly add in adverbs. It won't come easily to a lot of students, but this is an incredibly effective activity, increasing both an understanding of the different forms of a given word and its multiple uses as well as recognition that parts of speech change the way we can use a word.

Day 4 incorporates word sorts to promote active engagement and manipulation of words. They are especially valuable when students classify words by sounds, spelling patterns, and meanings (Templeton, 2012). It may be helpful to begin by utilizing closed sorts, in which you furnish students with a list of categories and then they classify words based on those choices. After they have gained experience with this activity, however, a more challenging version is the open sort in which students identify

TABLE 4.4 Word Sort Sample

Words Containing Two Syllables	*Words With Long Vowel Sounds*
reveal/local/crisis/persuade/ frantic/mutter/fracture	bravery/reveal/local/ discrimination/crisis/obligated/ amplify
Words Containing Three Syllables	
amplify/infection	*Words With Prefixes*
Words Containing Four Syllables	discrimination/infection
obligated	*Words With Suffixes*
Words About Health	bravery/discrimination/frantic/
fracture/infection	*Words That Express Stress*
Words That Are Opposite	discrimination/crisis/frantic/ fracture/infection
mutter/amplify	

as many categories as they can imagine. Table 4.4 displays an excerpt from a fifth-grade word sort.

By Day 5, students are equipped to progress to the "generative" level at which time they should be given opportunities to use the word lists in novel contexts. This may take place through an assignment of simply using the target words in single sentences or crafting stories that include all of the target words. Beck and colleagues (2002) suggest that students may be less likely to create generic sentences if they are given a stem statement using the target word and asked to complete it in a meaningful way. For example, "A *generous* man heard of a family who lost their home in a fire, so he . . ." Alternatively, students may be asked to respond to questions containing target words that help them to make personal connections, such as "Have you ever known anyone who was *generous*?" or "Can you describe a situation when you have been *generous* to others?" These personal responses encourage interactions with words in a much more student-centered approach (Beck, McKeown, & Kucan, 2002). Figure 4.3 shows an excerpt of student work using target words to craft an original mystery.

Whether these sample activities are used or others are developed, planning should take into account the principles of vocabulary instruction gleaned from decades of literacy research and ensure collaborative opportunities for students to focus on

> It was a dark night when an old man ran into the *local* police station and *revealed* that he had witnessed a robbery. He told the police officer that he felt *obligated* to report it.
>
> He kept *muttering*, "I know who did it! I know who did it!" Although the police officer tried to *persuade* him to identify the culprit, he refused.
>
> *Frantic*, the old man . . .

FIGURE 4.3 Student-Generated Writing

personalized vocabulary study that supports their learning in a seamless transition through association, comprehension, and generative knowledge levels. Adhering to this model offers the potential of closing the vocabulary gap in your classroom.

For primary students who are studying high-frequency words, Figure 4.4 illustrates sample activities that also follow the three levels of word knowledge but are more developmentally appropriate for emerging readers—with extensive experiences employing kinesthetic, hands-on tasks as well as multiple opportunities for students to write and explore language.

1. **Personal Dictionary:** Write the word in student's personal dictionary. Include a sentence in the entry as well as a student sketch—if possible. (If students can write their own sample sentence for the dictionary entry, then allow them to do so. If students cannot write their own sample sentence, write sample sentences for them to copy.)
2. **Word Sort:** Sort the words by the number of categories selected (your decision based on the skill level of your students). Students must sort the words and then write them in their notebook with the label of each sort written at the top of the sort.
   - Match cards whose word begins with the same letter or syllable.

- Match cards whose word ends with the same letter or syllable.
- Match cards whose word has a similar meaning.
- Match cards whose words rhyme.
- Arrange cards according to alphabetical order.
- Arrange cards according to the number of syllables in each word.
- Find cards with the long vowels.
- Find cards with short vowels.
- Find cards that describe an action (verb).
- Find cards related to people.
- Find cards that describe.
- Find synonyms, antonyms or homonyms.

3. **Kinesthetic Spelling:** Working in pairs, one student reads the high-frequency word. The other student spells it using some form of manipulative (magnetic letters, index cards, word tiles, sand, individual white board). After checking for accuracy, the student spells the word in his or her notebook. The students then switch, and the other student spells a word read by his or her partner. This continues until all of the words have been spelled by both partners.
4. **Sentence Building:** Craft a paragraph that contains the targeted high-frequency words students are studying. Write each sentence on sentence strips, using a different colored marker for each sentence. Cut up each sentence and give small groups time to reconstruct the sentences. After reassembled, each student should write the paragraph in their notebook.
5. **Student-Generated Text:** Write a text incorporating all of the high-frequency words currently being studied. Students should underline target words.

FIGURE 4.4 Vocab App Center Activities for K–3 Students

Vocabulary "In Action"

Mr. Clark is a fourth-grade teacher who has a number of students exhibiting a significant vocabulary deficit. He is concerned about their ability to read at grade level and observes many of them struggling to make meaning from text.

To address their needs, he utilizes personal vocabulary study with his class. On Day 1, during his whole-group instruction on vocabulary, he introduces five new words to his students. He writes them on the board, defines them in student-friendly language, and gives examples of them in context—often from his own life or from the students' background knowledge—as they take notes in their vocabulary notebook.

As students move to guided reading, Mr. Clark sees each group and briefly discusses the target words that individual groups will study based on their needs. Afterward, the students move to the Vocabulary APP center. As they think about the words they will be learning, they begin to sketch simple illustrations of what they see in their mind when they think of the words. One student draws a picture of a young girl hiding her face below the word *bashful*. The students keep all of their illustrations in their vocabulary notebook and bring everything with them the next day to whole group.

At Day 2, Mr. Clark asks his students to share their illustrations. As he comes to a new word, he asks various students to hold up their pictures so that everyone in the class can see them. Sometimes, he asks the class why they think the student drew that illustration and how it relates to the word. Other times, he asks a student to share an illustration, and the class has to guess what the picture represents. He follows the same procedure when groups come to guided reading. Taking just 2 or 3 minutes, the students share their illustrations from their individual lists. When they transition to the Vocabulary APP center, the students work collaboratively to identify synonyms and antonyms of the target words. Mr. Clark has a set of thesauri available to them, and encourages them to search for words online as well.

Mr. Clark creates a synonym/antonym chart on the board on Day 3. He asks students what synonyms and antonyms they

Vocabulary Development ◆ 73

found for each word. He takes his time to question students about how closely these words are similar and different, emphasizing that words are unique and may be used slightly differently in certain contexts. He repeats this process in guided reading. Students then move to the APP center and transform the target words into all of the possible word forms that can be used. This is their most difficult assignment. They sometimes do not know the new word forms. Working together, they use dictionaries and what they have learned in class this year to identify the noun, verb, adjective, and adverb form of each of the words. At the beginning of the year, Mr. Clark asked each group to focus on just one part of speech—so one group only looked at noun forms, another group focused on the verb forms, etc. After a few weeks of rotating their responsibilities and sharing their work during whole group, the class was prepared to complete the whole form.

It is this whole word form chart that Mr. Clark is working on during whole group on Day 4. He creates the template on the board so that everyone can see, with each of the target words already written. He calls on individual students to identify the word forms. As students answer, he draws their attention to the suffixes as a means to help them determine what part of speech the words may be. For example, when one student explains that *transformation* is the noun form of *transform*, Mr. Clark asks how she knows. The student replies, "I know it is a noun because *-tion* is a noun suffix." Students sometimes have incorrect entries in their chart, and Mr. Clark corrects their errors and gives them examples of how to use these news words in sentences correctly. While he repeats this work with the personalized words for each guided reading group, groups at the Vocabulary APP center compete against each other to create the greatest number of word sorts.

Day 5 is the most exciting day for Mr. Clark's students. They enjoy the competition of creating the most word sort categories. This week, the group that wins the competition has created 23 word sort categories. They have classified words based on number of letters, number of syllables, phonic generalization, morphemes, parts of speech, feeling words, words about people, words about places, words associated with happiness, etc. The group with the most sorts shares their work with the class, rationalizing to their classmates how they sorted the words. Any sort that cannot be rationalized may be challenged.

After sharing their sorts in guided reading for personalized vocabulary words, students move to the APP center where they are tasked with creating a funny story using all of their vocabulary terms. Although the parameters of the writing assignment differ each week, the students enjoy showing off their storytelling skills in different genres. Mr. Clark always gives his students a few minutes to share their stories with a partner; then, he asks students to nominate their classmates for the best stories. Students read their stories, and Mr. Clark posts the "Story of the Week" on his classroom bulletin board.

After several days of explicit instruction, collaborative tasks, and a structured feedback loop, students are ready to show what they have learned. To assess their mastery of word meanings, Mr. Clark asks his students to spell and define each term in their own words and use the terms in context (e.g., sentence or paragraph writing). With so much scaffolding and active engagement with vocabulary, his students feel confident and typically perform well—even weeks later as he re-visits the words.

Conclusion

How truly important is vocabulary study within literacy instruction? Tomlinson (1999) argues that it is so powerful that "vocabulary learning can't be left to chance because students' word knowledge affects whether they comprehend what they're reading, write effectively, and learn content-area information" (p. 225). Recognizing the influence vocabulary wields in students' literacy development as well as its place in a balanced literacy program, vocabulary plays a key role in the Core Literacy Block—especially in the use of personalized vocabulary study to meet the needs of all students in the classroom.

5

Strategic Reading Instruction

A balanced literacy program adheres to the five pillars of reading instruction. We have already discussed the role that phonemic awareness, phonics, and vocabulary plays in the literacy block. In this chapter, let's consider how comprehension and fluency join them to ensure that students develop the competencies necessary to read, write, and think in the 21st century.

Significance of Comprehension for Literacy Achievement

There is general agreement that comprehension lies at the heart of literacy instruction (Duffy, Roehler, & Mason, 1984; Durkin, 1993; Gambrell, Block, & Pressley, 2002). Unfortunately, looking again at Durkin's 1979 landmark study, only 1% of instructional time was devoted to comprehension strategies in elementary classrooms. She found that instruction followed a mention, practice, assessment cycle. Thus, teachers would mention a skill they wanted students to use, provide practice through worksheets, and then assess student ability to use that skill. What was

> "By third grade, most children who have not learned to wield comprehension processes enjoyably and profitably will have fallen so far below their peers that they will never regain their lost ground, even if they have decoding skills that are on grade level."
>
> *(Block and Pressley, 2002, pp. 42–43)*

missing, however, was the instruction needed to support the application of skills in any meaningful way. While this study was conducted several decades ago, explicit instruction of comprehension strategies have yet to be habituated into the instructional norm at the elementary level (Vaughn, Moody, & Schumm, 1998) or secondary level with research from Ness (2009) finding that after 2,400 minutes of secondary classroom observation only 3% was devoted to direct comprehension instruction.

In today's classrooms, comprehension instruction commonly stems from teachers who pose a series of basal-prepared or teacher-created questions after students have read a text—which typically serves to assess recall of a particular text, not teach global comprehension skills (Van Keer, 2004). Let's say that another way. Asking students comprehension questions after they have read a piece of text is not teaching comprehension. It is assessing it. Teaching comprehension entails showing students how to make meaning of text while they are reading—not just asking them questions after they have finished reading. Of equal concern is that by asking students comprehension questions after they have completed their reading, teachers are focusing on the recall of one specific text and not providing strategy instruction applicable to all texts. In 1997, Keene and Zimmerman challenged this approach, insisting that "children were not (and are not) learning to comprehend using this approach, and they certainly weren't becoming proficient, independent, confident, critical readers" (p. 16). Yet, this has continued to be the most prevalent form of comprehension instruction observed in classrooms.

Some educators operate under the belief that students will naturally develop comprehension skills without direct instruction on the part of teachers. Research, however, has proven that this is simply not the case (Wren, 2002). Direct instruction on strategies plays a central role in increasing students' comprehension (Harvey & Goudvis, 2000) especially for less-skilled readers and special needs students (Klingner, Urbach, Golos, Brownell, & Menon, 2010).

Similar to the vocabulary deficits discussed in Chapter 4, an over-emphasis on word identification skills in the primary grades produce students who by the fourth grade lack essential strategies to comprehend grade-level text (Fuchs & Fuchs, 2005). In fact, as early as third grade, students have already fallen behind so substantially that they may not be able to close the comprehension gap with their peers (RAND Reading Study Group, 2002). This points to the necessity of strategy instruction even in the early primary grades (Dooley, 2010; Eilers & Pinkley, 2006; Stahl, 2004). Interestingly, despite the obvious need for strategic reading instruction, even most secondary school reading classes neglect explicit comprehension instruction, concentrating primarily on literary analysis (Kelley, Lesaux, Kieffer, & Faller, 2010; Ness, 2009).

We know that proficient readers are decidedly strategic and seamlessly integrate multiple strategies to construct meaning from the texts they encounter (Huff & Nietfield, 2009). Not surprising then is that what characterizes many struggling readers is a lack of metacognitive skills essential for them to think about what they are reading and employ strategies to strengthen their ability to construct meaning (Eilers & Pinkley, 2006; Keene & Zimmerman, 1997).

Critics, however, often cite teaching strategies in isolation and the danger of encouraging memorization with no true grasp of strategies or how to use them reflectively as instructional concerns (DuCharme, Earl, & Poplin, 1989). In response to these well-placed misgivings, we encourage an explicit plan for strategy instruction that includes extensive interaction with targeted strategies and multiple experiences using them with authentic text—all under the guided support of teachers.

Comprehension APP Centers

Strategy instruction has emerged as a ubiquitous feature in anthologies, basals, and other commercial products. However, an examination of these programs reveal elements frequently absent from what we know to be "best practices" in literacy instruction, such as direct explanation, modeling, discussion, and application (Dewitz, Jones, & Leahy, 2009; Kragler, Walker, & Martin, 2005). Too often, commercial programs provide a brief discussion of a strategy, furnish questions or a worksheet for students, and then move hurriedly on to the next strategy to be learned. Sometimes these strategies are revisited later in the program . . . and sometimes they are never used again.

As we discussed in Chapter 2, a gradual release of responsibility characterizes this literacy block model. For students to succeed, they need direct explanation and modeling of strategies, guided practice, and opportunities for independent application. Within that paradigm, it is critical to remember that comprehension should not focus on individual passages—rather, it should provide a global perspective with strategies than can be used for all texts (Eilers & Pinkley, 2006). To ensure that students are thoroughly cognizant of how to apply strategies independently, follow a five-step process: 1) define the strategy explicitly; 2) explain why they are learning the strategy, focusing on its purpose and benefits to readers; 3) describe clearly how to use the strategy with real text; 4) clarify when and where the strategy can be used; and 5) discuss how to evaluate how effectively they used the strategy, along with fix-up strategies if they falter in its application (Winograd & Hare, 1988).

Student comprehension further improves when provided with peer discussion supported by instructional support and explicit direction (Diehl, Armitage, Nettles, Peterson, 2011; Keene & Zimmerman, 2013). When asked, 95% of educators believe that peer discussion provides new avenues for learning about literacy; however, only 33% voice its actual use in their classroom practice (Almasi, Arya, & O'Flahavan, 2001). This social interaction can easily be nurtured during whole-group mini-lessons, guided reading group discussions, and collaborative tasks at the APP centers.

Taking advantage of what we know to be effective strategy instruction, the Core Literacy Block emphasizes specific comprehension strategies that receive targeted, explicit explanation with opportunities for students to see these strategies modeled and explained during whole-group instruction. They practice these strategies in guided reading and apply them independently in the Comprehension APP center. Their work then drops into the feedback loop where they share their work from the APP center when they return to their guided reading group the next day. This cycle can continue until the teacher determines that students have mastered the strategy.

What does it look like in a classroom? Let's say that you are teaching your class about text features. You begin by defining what text features mean and illustrating several examples. You decide to focus student work on just one text feature at a time and devote the day's whole-group mini-lesson on headings, explaining their purpose and what readers can glean from them. As students transition to guided reading, you draw their attention to the headings in their text, asking them questions about what the heading tells them about the text. Before they leave your guided reading session, you pose three questions that they will answer in the Comprehension APP center: 1) What is the heading in the next section of our text? 2) How do you know it is the heading? 3) What information does the heading give the reader about this next section? Students will answer these questions in their reading notebook and bring their responses back with them to their next guided reading session with you.

Upon returning to guided reading the following day, students score each other's work. Why the students and not the teacher? While the teacher should certainly oversee their scoring and help them to express the thinking behind their scores, encouraging students to analyze written responses increases an objective understanding of the skills and strategies being studied while allowing them to internalize this insight in their own responses.

80 ◆ Components of the Core Block

Using a 2-point rubric, a student reads his or her response, and the other members of the guided reading group score the answer using cards with 0, 1, and 2 printed on them. Much like an Olympic event, each student displays the card that represents the score given to the response. While this is a simple activity, students love having their own individual cards to score. We use these cards every time that we work with students in guided reading. On one occasion, Betsy forgot to bring her cards with her to a class, and the students complained that they couldn't score without them!

As students score others' work, you may ask a particular student why he or she scored the response in the way he or she did. Then, ask the student who wrote the response if he or she agrees with the scores and how this feedback may change responses in future assignments. Figure 5.1 highlights a sample comprehension scoring rubric. This takes a bit of training, but within just a few days, students learn what each level of the score means and quickly begin to improve their answers. When working in classrooms, we have often had students stop reading their responses from the previous day. When we ask them why they have stopped, they will invariably mutter, "This isn't a 2. I forgot ___. Let me fix it, and then I can read it." So, it shifts from the need for us to explain why a student received a particular score, to classmates describing the characteristics of a particular score, to students writing their responses and being highly cognizant of what constitutes a response at varying levels of a rubric. Incorporating daily written responses with subsequent peer and self scoring, we have, without fail, watched students rapidly increase their ability to respond to text coherently and articulately.

Meanwhile, students love scoring their classmates' work. There is a sense of empowerment and accountability as students raise a card that denotes their evaluation of student work and then articulate the rationale behind their score. It only takes 2 to 3 minutes during guided reading. Yes. We said just 2 or 3 minutes. You may not hear every student or every

0   No response; Response not related to question; Response not legible 1   Response accurately answers the question; Incomplete sentence(s); No evidence from the text to support response 2   Response accurately answers the question; Complete sentences; Evidence from the text supports response

FIGURE 5.1 Comprehension Scoring Rubric

response—just a spot check. This spot check, however, allows you to tie the learning together within the context of peer support. Regie Routman (2000) maintains that "all learning involves conversation. The ongoing dialogue, internal and external, that occurs as we read, write, listen, compose, observe, refine, interpret, and analyze is how we learn" (p. xxxvi). Ketch (2005) sums it up even more simply: "Conversation is our connection to comprehension" (p. 9). These few minutes, then, are invaluable and should not be forgotten in the rush to get back to the text.

Notice that the feedback loop for comprehension does not return to the whole group. Rather, student feedback takes place during guided reading. Why the change for comprehension when word study and vocabulary both feedback to the whole group? First, students are functioning at diverse reading levels and reading different texts. Trying to pose questions with these varying texts can be confusing and not particularly effective. Looping back to texts appropriate to particular students is much more prescriptive to their needs. Second, strategy instruction requires substantial explicit instruction and modeling. You need the time set aside for mini-lessons to provide additional instruction. In the case of teaching text features, for example, you may spend a few days on headings before moving on to captions, sidebars, bold words, etc.

> " . . . reading comprehension improves when given the opportunity to meet with a small group of peers, with a concentration on reading and understanding, and with a teacher's focused instructional attention and explicit explanations."
>
> (Diehl, Armitage, Nettles, & Peterson, 2011, pp. 42–43)

Following this format, comprehension instruction takes place through explicit, direct explanation and modeling in the whole-group mini-lesson. It continues during guided reading with the teacher providing scaffolded support at varying levels needed by different guided reading groups followed typically by two to three comprehension questions. While these comprehension questions do not all have to center on the targeted strategy skill, at least one should. For example, you may elect to ask a summarizing question to determine if students understand what they have read thus far, a vocabulary question to ensure that students are applying word identification and context clue skills, and then a question centered on your target skill. You may also wish to re-visit a strategy to ensure that students are still using it actively and ask a question to verify its application in your students' reading repertoire. If your overriding concern is the target strategy, however, you may pose all of the questions on just that strategy. They will answer those questions in the Comprehension APP center and bring their responses to the next guided reading lesson where their classmates score and discuss their work.

The next big question is—how do you decide on what strategies to teach? If your school uses a commercial program, then you can certainly use that as a guide. Simply ensure that you provide quality instruction on the targeted strategy during whole group and follow the cycle outlined in this chapter. In other words, use the program as a resource and not as the sole basis of knowledge in the classroom. Other approaches include instruction based on universal comprehension strategies, standards-based strategies, prescriptive strategies, and integrated strategies. Let's examine these different options and see what they would look like in the classroom.

Universal Comprehension Strategy Instruction

Numerous authors have offered lists of universal strategies that have applications across grade levels and a range of texts (Duke & Pearson, 2002; Harvey & Goudvis, 2000; Stahl, 2004). Figure 5.2 highlights some of the strategies that they have proposed—many of which are included on multiple authors' lists. They assert that these strategies are vital if students are to become proficient readers. In fact, Stahl (2004) contends that "because effective readers use a variety of strategies to deal with troublesome text, teachers may want to move toward a repertoire approach as they become more comfortable with strategy instruction and its adaptation to the existing reading curriculum" (p. 606).

If this is an approach to which you feel an affinity, you probably ascribe to the philosophy that all students require a set collection of comprehension strategies, or thinking tools, as they encounter text. In this case, you want to ensure that your students don't just learn these strategies in isolation, but that they become intentional about their use when they read and eventually use them without prompting or conscious thought.

> # Universal Comprehension Strategies
>
> - Previewing
> - Story Structure
> - Determining Importance
> - Locating Details
> - Sequencing
> - Comparing and Contrasting
> - Summarizing
> - Predictions
> - Mental Imagery
> - Text Structure
> - Questioning
> - Drawing Conclusions
> - Monitoring Comprehension
> - Fix-Up Strategies

FIGURE 5.2 Universal Comprehension Strategies

Standards-Based Strategy Instruction

This approach links to standards-based instruction. Within this methodology, you provide instruction that is directly tied to reading standards. For example, if you are focusing on Common Core Standards, you would identify the benchmark expectations for your grade and then provide specific strategy instruction to support your students in mastering those grade-level expectations. For example, if you teach first grade, your students are expected to retell stories, including key details. If that is the goal, then you would offer strategy instruction on retelling narratives over the course of the academic year. (Appendix D lists the Common Core Standards for kindergarten through Grade 8 for Standards 1–9).

Prescriptive Strategy Instruction

Another approach is to plan for strategy instruction based on student deficits. If you select this methodology, then you tend to focus on the needs of your students and what you perceive as their missing skill sets. You determine key strategies that your students don't possess and then plan for ways to remediate those needs and bridge the gap of their deficits.

Integrated Strategy Instruction

The last approach is for those educators who feel compelled to embrace all of the approaches in tandem. If you select integrated strategy instruction, then you organize your literacy block to embrace universal strategies that all proficient readers should have, incorporate standards-based strategy needs that students are expected to master, and monitor your students for any deficits that become apparent when they are reading and responding to text.

This is a concentrated approach to strategy instruction and has the potential to improve students' comprehension of text on several fronts. It does, however, demand the most from you professionally. First, it requires a great deal of planning, substantial knowledge of comprehension skills and strategies, and coordination of ongoing instruction. Second, it can easily collapse into a strategies marathon with students feeling overwhelmed and unable to apply strategies in any meaningful way; thus, it is imperative that instruction be cohesive, logical, and explicit for student understanding—with sufficient time and opportunity to apply appropriate strategies with authentic text. Third, many of these strategies overlap among the different approaches, so you need to be knowledgeable about when and how to use them so that students don't just develop a broad repertoire of strategies, but also, more importantly, know when and how to use them independently.

One last caution about strategies instruction . . . recognize the difference between activities and strategies. We often talk with teachers about how they provide strategy instruction and what they describe to us are activities—not strategies. Activities are those tasks that you provide students to complete in your classroom or at home that may provide a structure to warehouse student work but don't offer them a tactic when they are reading and working independently. A strategy, on the other hand, furnishes a "systematic plan, consciously adapted and monitored, to improve one's performance in learning" (Harris & Hodges, 1995, p. 244). Need an example? When teaching her students about main ideas and supporting details, a third-grade teacher told us that she found a worksheet that had an umbrella upon which students would write the main idea of a text with little raindrops to represent the supporting details. Is that a strategy? Definitely not. It furnishes a place for student work, but students cannot use the imagery of an umbrella and raindrops to help them identify the main idea and supporting details of a text. Another example can be found during a graduate class that we taught on reading instruction, we met one-on-one with students—all tenured teachers from various school systems both public and private—to discuss their comprehension instruction and why they believed their students struggled so much with reading. They recounted multiple examples of their instructional practices and their student work. With so much emphasis on comprehension they couldn't understand why their students didn't improve. They were shocked when they realized that what they had described was a plethora of activities that kept students and themselves busy. Unfortunately, they could not identify one real strategy that they offered their students. So students completed assignments and answered questions, but they continued to struggle because they didn't have any strategies to help them comprehend text independently. It was an a-ha moment for these teachers, and it exemplifies the importance of strategy instruction.

So, what is an example of a strategy? For students who are learning about character analysis, we model how to search the text for clues about what the character says, what the character looks like, what the character feels, what the character thinks, and what the character does. Using all of that text-based information, students are then able to select a descriptive word for the character that takes into account all of the clues that the author left for the reader. That is a strategy that students can use independent of us whenever they are attempting to describe characters from narrative texts. You can read more about this strategy in the Comprehension Strategies "In Action" at the end of this chapter.

Let us be clear. There is nothing wrong with activities, just be sure that you also include specific strategies that students can take out of your classroom and use independently. The golden rule for comprehension instruction is to provide your students with concrete strategies that will make them independent of your support. Always ask yourself: What are they taking away from this lesson? It won't be a cute activity or a worksheet. It should be a tangible strategy that increases their self-sufficiency as independent readers and writers.

As we continue to delve into reading comprehension, let's look at the relationship between fluency and comprehension. In this next section, we will review fluency's effect on student ability to construct meaning as well as the role of fluency in the literacy block and how to integrate it seamlessly into daily instruction.

Fluency's Role in Comprehending Text

As a balanced literacy model, it is important to integrate fluency into core instruction. You may be wondering why we are discussing it here in a chapter devoted to comprehension and not in a chapter by itself. It is here for a simple but significant reason. Fluency cannot and should not be taken as an instructional goal isolated from the other pillars of balanced literacy. Of greater concern, fluency cannot supersede comprehension as the overarching goal of reading instruction. In too many classrooms, students' ability to read quickly has taken precedence over their ability to make meaning from the texts that they read so hurriedly. We do not provide fluency instruction for the mere sake of reading faster or to meet a pre-set number of words read per minute. If reading quickly is the only purpose of instruction, students will gain nothing and perhaps even lose in the process. Fluency should always be viewed as one part of the reading equation. More importantly, it must be regarded as a means to improve a reader's comprehension. Remember that fluency is just one facet of supporting students as they mature into capable readers.

Although discussed as early as Huey's (1908/1968) classic review of reading research, our modern interpretation of fluency comes from the seminal work of LaBerge and Samuels' (1974) automaticity of reading model, which asserted that skilled reading necessitated the transition of cognitive resources from lower-level word identification processing to higher-lever comprehension functions. More simply put, students who slowly and painstakingly decode one word at a time expend so much of their thinking on word-by-word reading that they cannot make meaning at the sentence or paragraph level. Students who read fluently do not need to expend so much of their thinking processes on word identification; rather, they can devote their cognitive efforts to making meaning.

Despite the solid research base supporting this correlation between fluency and comprehension (Burns et al., 2010; Griffith & Rasinski, 2004), fluency is most commonly assessed through oral reading fluency (ORF) rates that encompass only the speed and accuracy that students can call out words, which can lead to a grossly misleading estimation of a student's true reading ability. For example, students who are classified as "word callers" may achieve high ORF levels and yet have little understanding of what they read. This holds true for a range of students, including English language learners (Quirk & Beem, 2012). Conversely, some students progress more slowly through a text but comprehend at deeper, more evaluative levels. Basing a judgment solely on a student's ORF fosters erroneous conclusions about reading skills. A more exact assessment of students' reading comprehension would be to complete a timed reading followed by a brief retelling of the passage, thus ensuring that the student not only called out words but also, and more importantly, constructed meaning from those words.

Fluency is typically defined as comprising automaticity, accuracy, and prosody. In this context, automaticity refers to the ability to apply word identification skills without conscious thought while accuracy denotes that words are read correctly. Prosody relates to expressive reading which includes phrasing, intonation, and attention to punctuation—all of which demonstrates that students understand what they are reading. Although in recent years attention has been paid almost exclusively to accuracy and automaticity with reading rate scores coming to represent a student's ability to read well, it is actually prosody that is the most essential aspect of fluency as it is prosodic reading that directly correlates to comprehension. This can be observed when students display appropriate phrasing, attention to punctuation, rise and fall patterns in their speech, and meaningful expression compared to students who may be "accurately" and "automatically" reading but do so with no pauses between sentences and with no expressive quality in their voices that suggest they understand the meaning of the text. That said, accuracy and automaticity are simply not enough; fluency will not support comprehension if there is no prosody. To this three-part definition, then, must be added the commonly used analogy of fluency as the "bridge" between word reading to comprehension (Kuhn, Schwanenflugel, & Meisinger, 2010), and that bridge will not exist without prosody.

Fluency instruction also doesn't always begin in earnest until Grade 2 when students begin to shift from reading word by word to reading in phrases. It is our stance that fluency is a building process that does not just constitute words and phrases, rather, it is an inclusive, extended process that encompasses the alphabet, phonics patterns, morphological elements, and syntax. Thus, you cannot wait until a student is older to begin fluency instruction. By then, it may be too late. Rather, consider the need for fluency in identifying the alphabet, in developing a sight word vocabulary, in recognizing phonics patterns, in leveraging morphemic knowledge for word identification, or utilizing syntax when reading—with these skills being practiced, reinforced, and transformed into a practice that is accurate and completed with ease (Wolf & Katzir-Cohen, 2001). If students are learning the alphabet, for example, can they identify the letters accurately and automatically? If not, their struggle with fluency will begin at a very young age.

As with other aspects of the literacy block, fluency instruction should also follow a gradual release of responsibility: teach (whole-group instruction), practice with support (guided reading), and apply (APP centers). Begin by offering explicit instruction on what fluent reading entails so that students develop a metacognitive awareness of how to become fluent readers. Modeling fluent reading can take place in the whole-group mini-lessons. An initiating and ongoing support is the act of modeling fluency itself. Read alouds present excellent fluency experiences as teachers model what proficient readers sound like when reading aloud. Although you can incorporate read alouds into the whole-group comprehension mini-lesson framework, you may find it more beneficial to leave this time for more explicit teaching and read aloud outside the literacy block. This will be discussed at much greater length in Chapter 7 when we look at expanded opportunities for reading throughout the academic day.

After providing explicit instruction during whole group, students can practice their oral reading fluency in guided reading sessions through the use of flexible grouping. So while the activities described below are commonly used in whole-group settings, we recommend shifting them to guided reading sessions so that you can use them in a more targeted capacity to address the needs of particular groups of students. In your classroom, you may need to re-organize students based on their fluency needs; however, you may find your current groups share similar needs. During guided reading sessions, you can offer prescriptive fluency instruction based on student need as well as supply corrective feedback to provide individualized support, ensure greater participation, and increase motivation.

Now, let's take a look at some fluency activities that function not just in whole-group instruction but also can be integrated into guided reading. Your instructional task will be to select the one that best meets the needs of individual guided reading groups. As with all other aspects of the Core Literacy Block, it is not a one-size-fits-all approach. One group may be characterized as relatively fluent readers lacking prosody who would benefit from Readers Theater. Another may be struggling to follow punctuation cues as fluency markers that might be supported through echo reading. Yet another group may be so dysfluent that they cannot successfully read through a complete sentence without stopping and starting as they approach each word. Because they cannot chunk text, it may be most helpful to use the phrase-cued texts. So, while fluency may be the goal of whole-group instruction, the approaches to support students' fluency fluctuates based on individual need. We'll begin with a discussion about Readers Theater and move to progressively more supportive practices.

Readers Theater provides a brief text in the form of a script that students practice reading in preparation for an oral presentation. Readers Theater furnishes an authentic purpose for rereading and has been found to increase motivation to read as well as oral reading fluency—especially prosodic reading that increases a more meaningful understanding of text (Kuhn & Rasinski, 2015). Students can read and "rehearse" the script in guided reading and the Comprehension APP center and then put on the production during whole group or a guided reading session.

Shared reading provides an enlarged text (e.g., big book, text written on poster, or interactive white board) so that all students can see while the teacher models fluent reading with repeated readings and interactive experiences (Holdaway, 1979). Koskinen and colleagues (1999) developed a specific protocol for small-group shared reading using common texts that was modified to use within the guided reading session. Its structure contains five steps: 1) plan the lesson based on the observed needs of the small group; 2) introduce the book, highlighting print features and language patterns; 3) read aloud by the teacher, pointing at words; 4) reread text orally together; and 5) reread again for fluency—typically in pairs. Afterwards, the books are made available for later rereading. Although valuable for all students, shared reading is particularly helpful for struggling readers and English language learners (Allington, 2001; Drucker, 2003).

Another scaffolding activity is **choral reading** in which students read aloud in unison with the teacher from the same text, practicing accuracy (e.g., pronunciation), automaticity, (e.g., appropriate reading rate), and prosody (e.g., reading with expression). Afterwards, the teacher offers corrective feedback about troublesome words, phrasing markers (e.g., commas and periods) as well prosodic markers (e.g., question marks or exclamation marks), leveraging the experience to focus on reading with one voice.

In **echo reading**, the teacher reads aloud a brief passage, modeling phrasing and expression. Then, students "echo" back the same passage, mimicking how the teacher read. This allows a bit more support than choral reading as it affords students the ability to first hear the fluent reader before attempting the same passage independently. Although a simple activity, it has been shown to improve oral reading fluency (Shanahan, 2006).

Significantly dysfluent readers are characterized by short, choppy, word-by-word reading. **Phrase-cued text** is an activity to alleviate these weaknesses and support student reading through phrases and meaningful chunks. Phrase-cued text has been found to increase overall reading fluency (Rasinski, 1990/1994) as it shows students how to group words into phrasal units where the meaning of the text can be found. To prepare, select a brief text appropriate to the instructional reading level of the students and apply slash marks to the phrasal units. There should be one slash mark (/) between phrasal units and two slash marks (//) at the end of sentences. Distribute copies of the marked texts to the students. First, read aloud orally to the students, emphasizing the slash marks and how it dictates pauses in reading. Then, reread the text together, and finally, pair up students to read again. Figure 5.3 illustrates a sample of a phrased cued text.

Independent fluency tasks can be equally powerful and provide much-needed time for students to strengthen their reading. Within the Core Literacy Block model, students can take part in these activities during the Comprehension APP center. As with guided reading, the activities described below become increasingly more supportive. Let's begin with repeated re-readings—one of the most well-known fluency practices used in classrooms.

During summer / I like to fly kites / at the beach. // I also like / to make sand castles / and lie in the sun / with my mom. // This is my favorite time / of year. //

FIGURE 5.3   Phrase-Cued Text Sample

Repeated readings require students to reread a short text at their independent level multiple times until they reach a pre-established level of fluency. Researchers have consistently judged it to be an effective practice to increase oral reading fluency (Samuels, 1979/1988; Therrien, 2004). To prepare the Comprehension APP center for this activity, supply appropriate texts and timers for the varied small groups coming to the center. Once there, students work with partners. As one student reads the text, the partner sets the timer for 1 minute. When the timer signals the end of 1 minute, the partner counts the number of words read correctly in 1 minute (WCPM) and records it on a personal reading sheet. The student rereads the same text three to five times. Each time the partner times and documents the total number of words read in 1 minute. Then, the partners flip and complete the process again.

Assisted reading strategies offer another option, providing opportunities for students to listen to pre-recorded texts that they can mimic as they read along and is particularly helpful for less able readers who lack prosody (Flood, Lapp, & Fisher, 2005).

Students who do not improve fluency rates with ongoing practice may be experiencing processing speed deficits and might benefit from focusing on **increasing processing speed,** practicing letter naming drills or fast reading of phonics patterns (e.g., word families) to develop necessary automaticity and accuracy at a more foundational level (Welsch, 2006). To prepare the center, put words on cards and instruct students to read the cards as quickly as possible. Pairing processing speed drills with repeated readings and partner reading, Wolf & Katzir-Cohen (2001) found that students increased skills in word identification skills as well as fluency and comprehension.

It should be noted that although fluency instruction can be the sole focus when teaching comprehension, it is also possible to use fluency supports in a more responsive manner to attend to needs as they arise. For example, if you observe students in a guided reading group struggling orally to read a text, it may be helpful to include a fluency support activity. Within the course of reading the text, then, you may elect to add in choral reading

94 ◆ Components of the Core Block

of a few sentences or even stop at a particularly problematic sentence and create a phrase-cued text of that sentence. Once used, you can easily go back to reading the text as usual; however, students have had the benefit of guidance as they tackle a difficult text.

Now that we have reviewed how strategy instruction and fluency activities can work in tandem to improve reading comprehension, let's take a look at one classroom and how the teacher uses strategy instruction to support student learning.

Comprehension Strategies "In Action"

Ensuring that her students can make meaning from text is critically important to Ms. Banks. A third-grade teacher, her school system has embraced a standards-based approach in their literacy instruction, so she works hard to focus her teaching on Common Core literacy standards. Ms. Banks, however, is also concerned about some deficits that she has observed in her class and believes that she may have to remediate along with the grade-level instruction that she is providing.

For the next couple of weeks, Ms. Banks is focusing on narrative elements, specifically on character traits. She begins by writing the term "character traits" on the board and explicitly defining the term for her class. She then reminds them of several stories they have already read this year and encourages her students to describe some of the main characters, prompting them to explain how they came to those descriptions. As students struggle to articulate how they identify character traits, Ms. Banks illustrates a strategy to help them determine the traits of a particular character, explaining that sometimes an author may tell the reader what traits a character has but more often the author leaves clues for the reader to find. The task, then, is to know what clues to look for when reading a story. She goes on to enumerate the five kinds of clues on which she wants students to focus: 1) how the character looks, 2) what the character does, 3) what the character says, 4) what the character feels, and 5) what the character thinks. Using a picture book, she reads the story and pauses periodically to ask students what the character looks like, charting their responses on the board. At the completion of the read aloud, she asks students to consider what they noticed about the physical description of the character and summarize it within one descriptive word. She emphasizes that they can evaluate how well they have used the strategy by being able to present evidence from the text to support their answer.

As each guided reading group meets with Ms. Banks, she draws their attention back to the mini-lesson earlier in the day and reviews the five clues that readers can use to identify character traits. Using their guided reading books, she distributes sticky notes to each student. As they read the text, she instructs them to affix a note when they find a physical description clue and write down one word that summarizes what that description tells them about the character. After sharing their "evidence," she sends them off to the Comprehension APP center, telling them to think about all of the clues that they have found so far and tasks them to answer the following question: "How would you characterize ___? Use evidence from the text to support your answer."

The following day, Ms. Banks returns to the character traits clues strategy, asking student to define character traits and recount the five clues that readers can utilize to help them determine accurate descriptions of a character. During the mini-lesson, she talks about the textual clues that readers can find by looking at the character's actions in the story. Returning to the same picture book, she rereads the story, instructing her class to raise their hands when they hear an action that a character takes that helps them to understand the character better. When a student raises a hand and responds, she charts the character's action on the board. Afterwards, the students work to come to a consensus about a one-word description based on the details listed on the board.

Meeting again with her guided reading groups, Ms. Banks asks the students to share the responses to the question she posed, and classmates in each group score each other's work using a two-point rubric. Building off of the whole-group instruction, groups continue reading their texts and use sticky notes to mark passages in the text that refer to character actions. She then assigns each group to take the guided reading books with them and mark the next two pages for character actions as well as answer one question: "The author shows that ___ (character) is ___ (description). Write a paragraph telling how the character is ___ (description). Use specific details from the story to support your answer." Ms. Banks notices that one group is struggling to identify actions that are significant and are just listing everything the character does in the story. She waits to see their work the following day, but she plans on how to provide additional support for these students if necessary. Ms. Banks also anticipates that another group will stumble over a particular passage in their text that includes dashes. In preparation, she writes the sentence on a small white board and adds slash marks indicating where to pause. When they reach that passage with no indication of their awareness or meaning of the dashes, she explains why authors use dashes and how to read with them in a sentence, demonstrating with her slash marks. After students practice a couple of times, she shows them a new sentence with dashes and asks them to read it. Once she is confident that her students understand, she continues on with the text.

The next 3 days continue the format of the previous lessons. She reviews the strategy, rereads the story and applies a different clue to the story with students actively searching for evidence of the clues. This process also continues in guided reading sessions and APP centers. One group, however, exhibits an inability to identify key details, listing everything they found in the text. For these students, Ms. Banks added a prescriptive strategy—determining importance. She explains to the group that readers need to determine what's significant in a story. A simple strategy to do that is to focus on main events. Rereading a passage from their guided reading books, she asks the students to identify what the main events are in that excerpt. Once identified, she draws their attention to those events and asks them what the character is doing during those events. With that as an explicit strategy, she assigns the group to continue reading their text during the Comprehension APP center. This time, they are to write down the main events before they answer any other question about the highlighted clue.

As students continue to apply the character traits clues in their reading and responding about narrative text, Ms. Banks wants to increase her students' independent application of the strategy. The following week, she sets aside time during one of her mini-lessons for students to create life-size "characters." Giving each group long strips of butcher paper, they work together to draw an outline around one student from their group, forming the illustration of a person. Then each student is given a different colored marker. One student from each group draws a thought bubble above the character's head and writes the words "Thinks" above it. Another creates a speech bubble and writes the word "Says" above it. A third student draws a heart and writes "Feels," and a fourth makes a square near the feet with the word "Does" written near it. Finally, a student draws a rectangle vertically along the side of the butcher paper and writes "Looks like." The finished drawings are placed in the Comprehension APP center. In preparation for this activity, Ms. Banks selects a brief text for each group. After reading with each group and ensuring they understand the story, she sends them off to the APP center to complete the first part of the task—documenting each clue from the text onto their life-size character sheet. Students bring their life-size characters with them to the next day's guided reading group and explain where they found their clues. With all of their evidence in place, Ms. Banks instructs each group to write a paragraph responding to the question: "What word best describes the character? List details from the story to support your choice." Students must work together to settle on just one word that they believe best describes the character based on all of their clues.

During the next day's comprehension mini-lesson, Ms. Banks hangs up all of the life-size characters around the room, and students take a "gallery walk" to see all of the different sets of clues. Because groups had varied texts based on their instructional needs, the students have read different stories. Consequently, she asks each group to explain their character clues to the rest of the class. Without telling the class the one-word description they agreed on to represent the character, the other students offer character traits based on the clues the groups have documented. Ms. Banks finds this activity to be highly motivating and great practice for learning how to use the clues to establish an accurate character description. So, when not all of the groups get to share, she announces that they will finish their character clues tomorrow. Meanwhile, each group meets with her during guided reading to show her their group response based on the evidence that they listed on their life-size character sheet.

Ms. Banks continues to work with her students on story elements, but this series of lessons revolving around one specific strategy has strengthened her students' abilities to make meaning from narrative texts, draw conclusions based on textual evidence, and summarize key details—as well as to respond to text clearly and intelligently.

Conclusion

Reading comprehension remains the primary goal for literacy instruction. Unfortunately, it has slowly turned into read a story, ask a series of questions, give a worksheet, and repeat. Although strategy instruction is talked about, it has still not permeated into our daily practice. If students are to become independent readers and thinkers, they must be armed with the strategies that proficient readers possess.

What's more, fluency must function as a significant component of the literacy block. It cannot, however, take precedence over comprehension or focus so exclusively on accuracy and automaticity that prosody and its relationship to meaning-making suffers. Fluency should be viewed as yet another building block in the foundation of effective literacy instruction.

Taken together, strategy instruction and fluency activities work symbiotically to improve reading comprehension. They cannot be divorced from one another—without weakening both. Recognizing their unified strength ensures a powerful literacy program.

6

Writers' Craft

In the cacophony of calls for improved reading and math achievement, less thought is given to writing instruction—either as a goal in its own right for its ability to allow students to communicate their thoughts and ideas to others or as a means to support learning in the content areas (National Commission on Writing, 2003). This may be attributed to the fact that "people think of listening and reading, not talking and writing, as the core activities in school" (Elbow, 2004, p. 10). Despite the apparent disregard for teaching writing, the ability to write well remains a key marker of school achievement and eventually success in the workplace as today's world demands that "writing well is not just an

> "If students are to make knowledge their own, they must struggle with the details, wrestle with the facts, and reword raw information and dimly understood concepts into language they can communicate to someone else. In short, if students are to learn, they must write."
>
> *(National Commission on Writing, 2003, p. 9)*

option for young people—it is a necessity" (Graham & Perrin, 2007b, p. 3).

Significance of Writers' Craft for Literacy Achievement

What emerges from this neglect of writing instruction is a silent crisis involving students' inability to express themselves in written formats. Indeed, when students enter kindergarten there are already gaps in their literacy skills, and as early as the fourth grade, a majority of students displays an inescapable need for improvement in their writing skills (NCES, 2003). This presents a crucial need for educators to address writing problems in the early primary grades so that at-risk writers do not develop ongoing writing difficulties.

Despite the prevailing practice in schools to abandon writing instruction in favor of devoting more time to reading, we know that additional writing instruction actually produces increased gains in reading over just allocating more time to reading instruction (Weber & Henderson, 1989). One reason for this is that reading and writing are linked cognitive processes. Strengthen one, and you strengthen the other. For example, if students learn how to write a well-developed narrative, then they more easily recognize those same elements in texts they are reading and, importantly, are more capable to read them at deeper levels of comprehension. This can be seen in middle school classes that focus on the climax of stories. If students study how to craft a powerful climax in their own writing, then identifying one in literature is facilitated as they use the skills they learned in their writing pieces now in their reading texts. Similarly, when students are reading complex texts—be it in literature or in the content areas—providing opportunities to write about what they are learning allows them to process and articulate their understanding of the content, connect their prior knowledge to this new learning, clarify concepts with which they may be struggling, and in effect, actually increase their comprehension and retention of what they are reading.

In short, writing instruction is not just about becoming a better writer or a more concise communicator with others. Writing supports reading comprehension and learning in the content areas. Thus, by neglecting writing as an essential component of the language arts program, reading comprehension is also hindered. Just how does this relationship influence literacy achievement? Its strength lies in the reading-writing connection.

The Reading-Writing Connection

We have all heard the term *the reading-writing connection*. What, though, does that really mean? How important is this link, and how does it influence reading and writing achievement for students? These are some of the questions that we want to answer in this chapter as we begin to consider—just how important is writing?

Both reading and writing are based on the same alphabetic system. Thus, within the first year of schooling as students begin to develop their phonological skills in identifying sounds of letters, they also should receive complementary instruction in spelling so that as they distinguish isolated individual sounds they can also write these same letters (MacKenzie & Hemmings, 2014; Ritchey, 2008). The value of spelling was highlighted in the well-known national report, *Writing to Read*, in which the authors indicated that teaching spelling increased word reading skills in students Grades 1–5 and reading fluency of students in Grades 1–7 (Graham & Hebert, 2010). Simply put, if students can spell a word, then they can identify it when they are reading. Conversely, if they struggle to spell the word, they are less likely to recognize it within a passage.

Beyond basic skill development, reading and writing continue to operate in nearly tandem functions as writing about text supports student comprehension and learning of the text itself. Fordham, Wellman, and Sandmann (2002) make the case for merging reading and writing because they are reciprocal processes and "considering a topic under study and then writing about it requires deeper processing than reading alone entails" (p. 151).

This mutual dependency is also found in what impedes their progress. In reading, we know that a deficit of the foundational skills of phonemic awareness and decoding slow down reading fluency and, in turn, comprehension by the need for students to expend so much of their cognitive resources on word identification that they struggle to make meaning. Likewise, if students lack handwriting fluency and spelling skills, they will devote so much of their processing skills to basic transcription of individual words that they will falter when trying to express their ideas through writing. What happens, then, is if handwriting and spelling are not automatic, composing deficits occur (Graham, Harris, & Fink-Chorzempa, 2002; Jones & Christensen, 1999). Thus, students who struggle with word identification hesitate over words, reread words, and grapple with comprehension after devoting so much time and thinking with word-by-word reading, so do students who write at a slow rate and stumble over spelling words expend so much of their energies on this low-level processing of transcribing words to paper that they may have little effort left to exert on composing as they often forget their initial ideas or become too frustrated to continue with this level of effort.

We know that the amount of time devoted to writing has a positive influence on reading comprehension (Graham & Hebert, 2010), but this in itself can even be problematic as a national study of elementary teachers revealed that there is significant variation in instructional practice, for instance, teachers indicated that the amount of time devoted to composing activities in their classrooms ranged from 0 to 380 minutes with an average of 105 minutes for the entire week (Graham, Harris, Fink-Chorzempa, & MacArthur, 2003). If we consider the average school year, that suggests that students spend a total of 63 hours in writing instruction for an entire academic year! Similarly, upper elementary teachers report that they devote a mere 15–20 minutes a day on writing and place little emphasis on analytical writing (Gilbert & Graham, 2010; Graham & Hebert, 2010). In contrast to these times, students should actually spend 45–60 minutes in daily writing activities in order to develop the necessary skill sets in writing. This change would revolutionize writing in your classroom to generate an amazing 300 hours devoted to writing per year! How can you make this happen? Ensure that you have a dedicated, protected time set aside for writing every day. Also, don't restrict instruction only to the traditional writing period but expand it to writing in the content areas and encouraging students to write for multiple purposes (Graham & Perrin, 2007a).

That brings us to another common expression in the education field that is "writing to learn." It is a ubiquitous phrase typically employed as students transition from primary to intermediate grades to denote the power of writing in content areas as students mature—yet strangely, it is not typically integrated in daily instructional practice. What does "writing to learn" mean in the reality of your classroom? Theorists, researchers, and expert practitioners have long argued that engaging students to write about informational topics they are studying (e.g., science and social studies), allows them to solidify and augment their learning. In a meta-analysis of empirical research conducted on the topic, Graham and Hebert (2010) determined that comprehension improved in Grades 2–12 when students wrote about what they read, and these benefits were consistent for struggling readers and writers as well.

So, it is abundantly clear that reading and writing are inarguably linked. With an appreciation of the power these two inverse processes have to increase achievement in both fields of studies, the next question is how should writing instruction be structured, and how does it function in relationship to the Core Literacy Block?

To answer that question, we must be mindful that another similarity that writing shares with reading is that student self-efficacy plays a vital role in their motivation as well as their ability to act independently. Sadly, if students do not see themselves as successful writers, their writing performance suffers (Klassen, 2002). This process begins early in a student's academic career and gradually worsens over time (Knudson, 1995). This is one of the principle reasons that we believe that prescriptive writing instruction is essential if students are going to receive the writing support they need and continue to build their skills over time. This is also why writing must be protected and why we will show you in the rest of this chapter how to provide prescriptive writing instruction for your students, using a number of strategies, including guided writing groups.

Integrating Writing Instruction in the Classroom

Integrating writing into your classroom practice requires intentional, thorough planning and a commitment to the power of writing to effect change within the academic performance of your students. How do you start? It all begins with eight key elements of effective writing instruction.

Intentional Planning. When we talk about the Core Literacy Block, we emphasize that every aspect of your work with students should have a specific, targeted instructional purpose. This same degree of focus is essential in writing if you want to see your students become proficient writers. There must be clear and deliberate planning, but it must also—just as in reading instruction—be flexible to meet the specific needs of the students in your class. So, whether you have a writing program already in place, you follow the academic standards your school system has adopted, or you have full autonomy to teach writing based on your professional expertise, be certain that you have a plan for what you want your students to be able to do as writers and targeted lessons that will scaffold students to this ultimate objective. This is the first rule for effective writing instruction: If you don't have a plan and a discernible objective, your students aren't going anywhere!

Eight Key Elements of Effective Writing Instruction

- Intentional planning
- Explicit instruction
- Modeled writing
- Shared writing
- Guided practice
- Independent practice
- Specific instructional purpose for every mini-lesson generated from error analysis of student writing
- Ongoing conferences

With a writing plan in place, consider how you will deliver instruction. Students need comprehensive support when they are composing texts, and this is accentuated in the scaffolding afforded through guided writing (Gibson, 2008). Guided writing functions much as guided reading does in the traditional literacy block. Students are grouped flexibly together with the teacher meeting with them about their writing, following a gradual release of responsibility that follows a predictable pattern—explicit instruction, modeling, guided practice, and independent practice. This will require you to assess your students' writing skills and group them based on their current skill set. While it should be flexible to allow students to move when needed, grouping students permits them to work collaboratively and economizes your efforts as you work with students who share comparable skills.

With this organizational structure in place, you can offer prescriptive, personalized instruction in writing in much the same way as you do with reading. After delivering whole-group instruction (i.e., explicit instruction, modeled writing, shared writing), students should then move to their writing groups. Just as students come to you for guided reading every day, they also come to you for guided writing. When they are not with you, they continue to compose their pieces—wherever they may be in the writing process.

Explicit Instruction. Writing should not be a mysterious process. In Chapter 5, *Strategic Reading Instruction*, we demonstrated the importance of strategy instruction in building comprehension skills for your students. In the same way that you provide strategies to support reading growth, incorporate specific strategies for writing as well. For example, if students are struggling with effective leads, emphasize specific categories of leads which they can use in their own writing, like beginning with a statistic, a question posed to the reader, or a dialogue between two characters, and then furnish scaffolded support to lead them to the independent use of these strategies in their own writing.

A common mistake that we make in our classrooms is narrowing our instructional focus. We emphasize taking notes, writing summaries of texts, and answering short-answer questions

(Applebee & Langer, 2011)—all of which is important—but sometimes to the detriment of longer, more creative pieces. Equally worthy is the need to learn how to write in different genres and for different purposes. To accomplish this range of writing proficiencies, students need specific strategies to write effectively in each of these contexts.

Providing explicit instruction for students about key strategies that good writers use should be the primary mode of delivering instruction. Please note that strategy instruction is not geared exclusively to upper-grade students. Strategy instruction can be used with very young children—beginning in first grade (Gibson, 2008). Even at this early age, you can provide strategies on how to construct a logical sentence or organize sentences into a coherent paragraph.

Modeled Writing. Modeling often works jointly with direct instruction. Before you can task students to write in a particular genre or for a distinctive purpose, you first need to show them a model of what a well-crafted piece of writing would look like so that they have an exemplar and a clear understanding of your instructional expectations. Without this, students, even high-achieving students, often flounder. Too often we assign our students writing tasks without first defining for them what these products will look like and how their particular writing pieces can become more polished by analyzing how good writers write.

One powerful way to provide this kind of direction comes from the use of mentor texts. Defined in 2007 by Dorfman and Cappelli, mentor texts are "pieces of literature that we can return to again and again as we help young writers learn how to do what they may not yet be able to do on their own" (pp. 2–3). In addition to these professional examples, keep in mind that you also serve as a mentor to your students and that your writing can demonstrate real-world examples. It can be particularly helpful to model writing the piece in front of your class in a writing think aloud so that your class comes to recognize what authors "do" and how they can integrate those thinking processes in their own writing. In short, "our children need to stand next to us and see how we write" (Gallagher, 2011, p. 8). So, whether you use a published work or one of your creations, the use of mentor texts can be a strong support for students as they look to models for their own writing.

Shared Writing. Shared writing offers another scaffold for students in which you compose a piece of text together with your students. Making the writing process both concrete and transparent, discuss the topic, audience, and format as a point of beginning for good writing. As you compose, concentrate on the collaboration aspect of this activity. Don't lead the writing. Instead, ask probing questions, guiding them through the writer's world with queries like, "Is there a better word we can use here?" or "Do we need to add more elaborative detail in this paragraph?"

This experience can be completed in as briefly as 5 minutes or may carry over to the next day. It depends on the length of the piece you are attempting and if you want to complete just a first draft or revisit it for revisions and edits. For young students, however, center attention on just one or two key instructional points.

Guided Practice. Strengthened with these scaffolds, students should be prepared to apply what you have taught them. They will still, however, greatly benefit from the gradual release of responsibility that we discussed in Chapter 2. With this in mind, assign students to begin your writing task. Remember that this is the most critical stage when students need the most reinforcement. This can come in a number of different ways: creating paired writing pieces, collaborating with peers, and eventually writing independently. In each of these configurations, you will continue to meet with students in guided writing groups. You can use all three of the forms of guided writing as a continuum of decreasing scaffolds and increasing responsibility, or you can select any of the three that you feel would benefit your students the most. You decide based on the needs of your students for the particular assignment, however, struggling writers have greater support when transitioning through several forms of guided writing in their attempts to hone their skills and increase their self-efficacy. Figure 6.1 illustrates this gradual release of responsibility in writing.

Let's go back to our example of focusing on writing leads. It may be helpful initially to pair students to craft different examples

108 ♦ Components of the Core Block

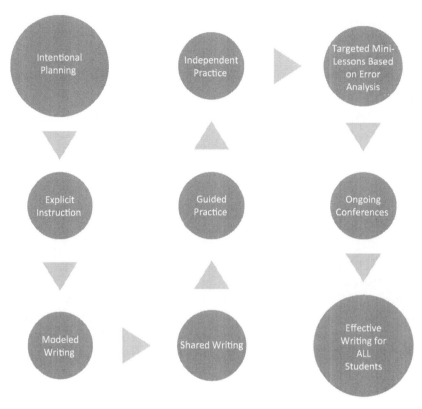

FIGURE 6.1 Gradual Release of Responsibility in Writing

of leads so that they have someone with whom they can clarify their understanding, practice their ideas in relative "safety," and gain confidence. On another day, you may allow them to collaborate on the initial ideas but be responsible for writing their own leads. After writing with support from their peers, they should, at the next lesson, be able to craft their own leads and write independently. Using this format slows the instructional process down, but it strengthens the likelihood that your students will master the skills you are teaching and assimilate them naturally in their writing repertoire. Also, consider the possibility of utilizing word processing programs during their independent writing so students develop their keyboarding skills, view their writing in a more professional manner, and more easily revise and edit their work.

Independent Practice. As students transition to independent writing, they should utilize the skills they gained during guided practice. Remind your students that good writers read their work and reflect on both the content as well as their writing style. When encouraging students to engage in that same process, it is helpful to provide them some key points to consider when reviewing their paper as a means to guide the process. Be sure to build this into your instructional time so that students realize its importance to you as well as its value to good writers. It is useful to ask students to share either with a partner or with the class so that they hear others' thoughts as well as offering you an opportunity to be cognizant of your students' perceptions about the task and themselves as writers.

Targeted Mini-Lessons. At this stage, take the time to assess your students' writing thoroughly. What errors are you finding? Are there patterns in their deficits? What are next steps in their writing? Answering these questions will take you to your next instructional move—targeted mini-lessons. Provide lessons linked to your learning objective, but your scrutiny of where students are struggling directs you to what your students' most pressing needs are on a day-by-day basis and leads you to targeted mini-lessons (e.g., capitalization, subject-verb agreement, verb tenses, paragraph organization, elaborion, word choice, voice, etc.). Using this information allows you to offer prescriptive mini-lessons of 5–10 minutes at the start of the writing lesson on a range of writing and mechanics concerns. Then, you can return to the guided writing process and have them practice these targeted skills or continue on to independent writing and have them apply the skills in the authentic context of their own writing. It is your choice . . . grounded in the needs of your class.

The issue of grammar always arises when discussing writing instruction. Rather than the contested practice of grammar worksheets with many in the educational field arguing that it has no meaningful effects on student writing, contextualize grammar instruction in writing itself. In place of the traditional grammar lessons that are taught in isolation outside the sphere of real writing, embed grammatical study within student writing and center the content of this study on the identified needs of students that can have a marked influence on student writing. In this approach, grammatical study is also based on error-based instruction developed by analyzing student writing. Prepare targeted mini-lessons and contextualize grammar in the revising and editing portions of the writing process so that students can see the importance of grammar within their own writing.

Ongoing Conferences. Student conferences can also help your students make substantial gains in their writing skills. When you meet with students during guided writing times, those conversations tend to be more general to the group. You also need time to talk with students one-on-one about their individual needs. You can conference at any time during the writing process, but it will be most effective during the revision stage when they are in the midst of their independent writing and may need direction to sharpen their pieces. To transition from guided writing groups to conferencing is relatively simple. Instead of taking groups, students continue to write as you meet briefly with individual students.

Prior to conferencing, put some preliminary expectations in place. To begin, make sure that your conferences entail no more than 5–10 minutes to ensure that you have an opportunity to talk with all of your students over the course of a given assignment. This time frame tends to keep you and your students focused on the objective, and you ensure that every student is receiving the prescriptive, personalized support they need. Also, students can often become discouraged and frustrated when they feel overwhelmed with the number and type of criticisms directed toward their writing. A common problem is that when teachers tend to focus more heavily on grammatical aspects of a text over the ideas and content expressed, they communicate, however inadvertently, that ideas are secondary to correct grammar.

To counter this problem, focus your conferences around a "pre-established task" or "genre-specific criteria" in which there is a balance between genre, content, organization, and mechanics (Lee, 2011). While you can certainly use a commercial rubric, you can just as easily construct one specifically aligned to your writing assignment. Simply review your assignment expectations and any mentor texts you are providing students, and from there list the key elements by which you would deem a piece effective. By expanding your focus to content and organization as well as the particular genre in which students are writing, you will not spotlight your attention so heavily on mechanics.

It is also advantageous to maintain a writing conference log. First, it allows you to ensure that you are meeting with all of your students equally. Second, it documents what aspects of the writing process each student is focusing on throughout the academic year so that you monitor growth. Third, the log adds accountability to your conversations so that both you and your students are reminded of the writing goals set at each conference. If, for example, you meet with a student who is struggling to use quotation marks correctly and you make that the goal for that particular student, then the next time you meet that will be the beginning of your dialogue. In this way, conferences are not transitory but maintain an enduring marker of the student's skill set.

After teacher-student conferencing has become habituated into classroom instruction, slowly transition into adding peer conferencing as well. This form of conferencing, in addition to your own individualized discussions, offers key benefits to student writing and has been consistently championed by researchers as providing much needed support to student writers, creating a context for their writing to be utilized as communication, to develop their knowledge of different writing genres, and to give them the language they need to talk about writing (Hoogeveen & van Gelderen, 2013). It is also another illustration of the gradual release of responsibility model. The goal is not for you to be the holder of all knowledge—but for your students to become independent of you!

Following these steps will lead you to an instructional plan for your writing program that supports students academically and improves their self-worth as writers. With this model in place, your students are on their way to becoming proficient and confident writers.

Writers' Craft "In Action"

In the pressure to raise his reading scores, Mr. Empson has often dropped his writing focus so that he could spend more time with his eighth graders on reading. This year, he has decided to provide a dedicated writing time as well as connect his writing instruction to real texts and topics his class is reading in literacy as well as in their science and social studies classes.

Using the academic standards his school has adopted, he has devised a plan that ensures that he will teach the major concepts that his eighth graders should master. In this particular unit, he is focusing on argumentative writing. He has provided a number of argumentative mentor texts for students to read and analyze, identifying key components that authors use to craft effective arguments. Students have also spent several days learning about the concept of claims—both identifying the claims that authors make when crafting arguments as well as practicing their own skills in developing effective claims. Mr. Empson now wants them to focus on providing grounds, or support, for their claims.

He begins by reminding his class that claims form the underpinning of arguments and should be based on conclusions drawn from what they have read about a particular topic—not opinions they cannot substantiate. A claim should also offer the potential of opposing points of view; otherwise, there would be no reason to argue for a belief or interpretation. He goes on to explain that in order to make a claim, the writer must have the "grounds" to support it. Mr. Empson explains grounds are also referred to as "support" or "facts" and cautions his class that without grounds to support a claim, the argument will fail. After highlighting several ways to provide grounds to a claim, such as evidence from texts, expert opinions, statistics, and facts, he tells his class that for the next few days they will concentrate on lifting evidence from text as explicit grounds for selected claims.

Because his students are studying the origins of American democracy in social studies, he selects three brief texts that address modern democracies and the issue of voting. After reading and discussing each of the texts, he makes the claim that voting is a human right. Then, he models for students how he identifies passages that support this claim and demonstrates how to embed these ideas in his writing as well as how to cite them so that he honors the work of others. He also provides time for shared writing as a "trial run" using this strategy.

Transitioning to their guided writing groups, he tasks his students to find the grounds to make the claim citizens should be required to vote by law. Working with a partner, each student searches through the documents to locate evidence that backs up that claim and drafts a single, collaborative piece. Mr. Empson meets with each guided writing group over the course of the following days to support their work and provide feedback. For students who are struggling, he provides them highlighters to distinguish between evidence that supports a claim and evidence that would dispute it and may better be used in a counterargument. This work continues when he asks students to collaborate on finding evidence that would back up the claim that when voting a representational democracy is more powerful than a direct democracy. This time, though, he instructs his class that they can work together to locate the evidence, but they must write their own individual paragraphs. As Mr. Empson continues to meet with his guided writing groups, he assigns the last mini-task in this section of his unit and reminds his class that they should work independently on this assignment. He poses the claim that voting is the most powerful method to effect change in a democracy.

As the class begins to work on this piece, he encourages his class to reflect on the expectations for this piece, for example, a clearly stated claim, clear organization and focused purpose, evidence lifted directly from the provided texts, correct citations, and an awareness of mechanics. Although he has a range of student performance levels, he does notice that many of his students do not cite their referenced texts correctly. Recognizing that this is an ability they must have in middle school, he presents a mini-lesson about citations and encourages them to use what they have learned in their writing for this assignment. Meanwhile, students also schedule times to conference with him. During this time, he discusses particular strengths illustrated in each piece as well as a focus skill that he recommends for each student.

Although Mr. Empson only concentrated on one element within an argumentative essay, he is pleased with his class progress as he continues to scaffold their understanding of key concepts in this genre of writing. After strong instructional support, assisted practice, and ongoing feedback and conferences, his students are grasping the concepts and exhibiting confidence in their writing. He has also noticed that his students are now able to identify the same elements of argumentative essays that they are learning about in his writing class when they read editorials, speeches, and arguments in reading, science, and social studies. He is seeing the results of his planning, his scaffolding, and his renewed commitment to connect reading and writing together!

Conclusion

Reading and writing have been consistently linked in research and in analyses of student academic performance. Unfortunately, it has often not been valued in classroom practices. Forging this connection and leveraging these inverse skill sets to boost the other increases competencies in both domains. Writing should be taught in tandem with reading beginning in the first year of instruction when students begin to acquire the alphabet. What's more, just as in reading instruction, students will benefit greatly from a gradual release of responsibility with structured supports in place. Writing has the potential to have a significant influence on students' literacy skills—it just needs to be integrated into instruction as a meaningful component of literacy and content learning.

7

Expanded Reading Opportunities

Adults are reading less every year. This holds true for children as well—with a disturbing trend of less and less recreational reading as children mature (Common Sense Media, 2014; National Endowment for the Arts, 2007). Beyond the obvious aesthetic benefits, reading for pleasure is associated with improved academic achievement and increased reading and test scores. With these advantages in the balance, how do you combat this decreasing desire to read for personal enjoyment?

> "In learning to read it is true that reading practice—just reading—is a powerful contributor to the development of accurate, fluent, high-comprehension reading. If I were required to select a single aspect of the instructional day environment to change, my first choice would be creating a schedule that supported dramatically increased quantities of reading during the school day."
>
> *(Allington, 2001, p. 24)*

It is an uncomplicated answer: additional engaging opportunities for reading in school to offset the loss of reading volume out of school as well as an introduction to students to the real joy of reading texts of their choice and discussing their reading in social interactions with peers and teachers. Beyond the protected time set aside for the literacy block, students need authentic contexts and environments to apply what they have learned in the literacy block—during read alouds, independent reading, and book groups.

Significance of Expanded Time for Student Reading on Literacy Achievement

Augmenting the amount of time designated for print experience and reading in school has a multitude of benefits that encompass every aspect of literacy development, including phonemic awareness, phonics, vocabulary, comprehension, and fluency. Let's begin with phonemic awareness.

Selecting read-aloud books that encourage students to play with language bolsters their development of phonemic awareness. At the onset, the act of reading aloud illustrates to young children that speech streams are comprised of units of sound that correlate back to printed language. Then, if chosen with phonemic instruction in mind, some texts can even offer fun, engaging experiences that lend themselves naturally to sound identification and manipulation. Yopp (1995) presents a bibliography of books that create opportunities especially well suited to this endeavor.

As students transition from phonemic awareness to phonics, a common criticism of phonics instruction is the potential to descend into isolated skill development—more commonly referred to as "drill and kill"—with no relation to authentic text. This concern can be negated, however, by offering reading experiences in tandem with explicit phonics instruction and guided practice with decodable text. Students further benefit from hearing texts that are more challenging than they read independently. In fact, as readers mature, they will profit even more from read aloud experiences with meaningful literature following these prerequisite skill-based activities.

A mainstay of reading instruction for all grades, vocabulary remains a key focus of the literacy block. Nevertheless, incidental learning still provides a substantial source of vocabulary acquisition. How significant is this? Cunningham and Stanovich (2001) explain it using an extrapolation of student test scores:

> the average child at the 90th percentile reads almost two million words per year outside of school, more than 200 times more words than the child at the 10th percentile, who reads just 8,000 words outside of school during a year. To put it another way, the entire year's out-of-school reading for the child at the 10th percentile amounts to just two days. (p. 141)

Thus, it becomes abundantly clear the consequence additional reading has on vocabulary acquisition as well as how alarming a deficit may be on academic growth. Additional reading experiences, then, furnish much-needed time and contexts to expose students to more varied and complex vocabulary (Beck & McKeown, 2001) as "reading aloud and facilitating text-based discussions about words provide contexts and opportunities for children to learn new words before they have the reading skills necessary to acquire vocabulary independently" (Santoro, Chard, Howard, & Baker, 2008, p. 398).

Similarly, the amount of time spent in reading experiences has a considerable effect on students' fluency—especially for struggling students who need so desperately to avoid falling further and further behind their peers. Allington (2001) even argues that without students reading voluntarily, there is little hope that they will become proficient readers. This can be seen in empirical studies that reveal that students who are encouraged to read for pleasure outperform students who follow only a traditional reading program (Krashen, 2004).

As the embedded purpose for all reading instruction, comprehension builds off the other components of balanced literacy. This same relationship is found when providing additional reading experiences. Reading aloud to students provides them a natural scaffold to approach text and supports them as they attempt to think about text at a deeper and more reflective level, in effect, to develop more advanced comprehension skills. These gains are further augmented through independent reading and book clubs (Lapp & Fisher, 2009).

Indeed, the three kinds of expanded reading opportunities that we will discuss in this chapter—read alouds, independent reading, and book groups—are so powerful that they comprise three of the six recommendations that Allington and Gabriel (2012) list for effective reading instruction that "every child should experience every day." Let's begin by looking at read alouds and what they offer students.

Read Aloud

Read-aloud experiences enhance a number of key reading achievement goals, including print awareness, incidental word learning, and comprehension (Dennis & Walter, 1995; Levy, Gong, Hessels, Evans, & Jared, 2006; Santoro et al., 2008; Vadasy & Nelson, 2012). In fact, Anderson and colleagues (1985) made the case that "the single most important activity for building the knowledge required for eventual success in reading is reading aloud to children" (p. 23), and those benefits extend to middle school students—especially in the areas of motivation and engagement (Albright & Ariail, 2005; Robb, 2000)—despite the fact that Serafini and Giorgis (2003) contend that in many classrooms "as students progress through the elementary grades, they encounter fewer and fewer opportunities to hear stories, see demonstrations of reading aloud, to talk about what has been read aloud, and to enjoy literature with their fellow classmates" (p. 7).

Despite their potential to produce solid increases in literacy learning, "empirical evidence indicates that the effectiveness of read alouds depends on how teachers read to students" (Brabham & Lynch-Brown, 2002, p. 465). Too often read alouds lack substance, as can be illustrated in a study of 537 classrooms that revealed that the average read-aloud experience followed a predictable pattern.

> The classroom teacher reads to students from a trade book for a period between 10 and 20 minutes. The chosen literature is not connected to a unit of study in the classroom. The amount of discussion related to the book takes fewer than 5 minutes, including the talk before and after the reading. (Hoffman, Roser, & Battle, 1993, p. 500)

Additional research indicates that questions posed during read alouds commonly relate to clarifying unfamiliar vocabulary or content and responding to detail-oriented questions (Beck & McKeown, 2001).

More effective talk stemming from read alouds, however, centers on helping students to consider the most important ideas of the text and not on simple retrieval questions based on literal recall. This can be viewed through the lens of two particular characteristics of high-level read alouds: interactive discussions and interpretative meaning. First, select interesting texts as the impetus for students to engage with the content and the author. Second, do not lead a question-answer pattern that volleys back and forth between you and your students, focusing on low-level comprehension and recall questions. Instead, encourage students to think about the text at more interpretive and reflective levels.

How do you ensure that your read aloud is not just appealing to students, but also instructionally rigorous? Begin with the book selection. Although sometimes it is enjoyable to read aloud in celebration of a holiday or just for a good read, for the majority of the time, choose a book based on its service to your instructional needs (Santoro et al., 2008). Search for a quality text that lends itself to grade-level curriculum, a current instructional objective (e.g., strategy application), as a link to other texts or topics, or as an introduction or extension of content area study (e.g., science or social studies). Also, don't forget to include a healthy diet of nonfiction materials—not just narratives. When making the selection, ensure that you have an explicit instructional purpose. That said, reading aloud is to be enjoyed by students. So be sure to preview the text and practice reading it prior to reading in front of your class so that your reading is well presented and holds their attention. Once begun, stop at intermittent points to model your thinking as well as to pose reflective, analytical questions about the text (Albright & Ariail, 2005). Following these guidelines will ensure a successful read aloud for you and your students!

In integrating read alouds into the academic day, educators have traditionally placed them within the literacy block. Despite this prevailing practice, we recommend that you place read alouds outside the literacy block. Why? After many years in K–8 classrooms, we have consistently observed teachers devoting 20–30 minutes to a single read aloud. While we don't disagree with an extended experience with a text, what alarms us is that teachers invariably say that they have to "drop" something from their literacy block in order to have the time needed for a read aloud. That loss of instructional time concerns us greatly. Meyer and colleagues (2001) highlighted this practice in a study when they found negative relationships between the amount of time teachers spent reading aloud and reading achievement. It was a surprising result, and the researchers posited that the effects were due to "displacement theory" in which the teachers who devoted the most time to read alouds spent the least time with instructional activities positively correlated to reading achievement. Thus, explicit instructional time was lost, and students suffered.

Some of our fondest memories are reading aloud to students. We have had students so engrossed in a story that they have begged us to continue reading. With one particular middle school class, Betsy had to lock her read aloud book in a filing cabinet every afternoon so that students could not read ahead to find out what happened in the cliffhanger from that day's reading. When you have to lock up a book, you know your students are hooked on reading!

Independent Reading

Silent reading. Free reading. Voluntary reading. Leisure reading. Whatever you call it, what we refer to as independent reading is a vital feature of a balanced literacy program with researchers habitually noting its association to increases in word recognition, vocabulary acquisition, fluency, comprehension levels, and motivation (Allington, 2009; Morgan, Mraz, Padak, & Rasinski, 2009; Reis, Eckert, McCoach, Jacobs, & Coyne, 2008; Vadasy & Nelson, 2012). In a landmark international study, Postlethwaite and Ross (1992) reported that the third highest predictor of reading achievement across the participating nations was reading at school. In fact, Dr. Lyman C. Hunt (1984), credited for developing the concept of silent reading in the 1960s, argued that in the context of teacher's practice, silent sustained reading should be viewed as "the pinnacle of achievement with regard to teaching skillful reading" (p. 192).

Like read alouds, independent reading is a popular activity among students—both at the elementary and middle school level. A study of approximately 2,000 middle school students revealed that independent reading was the first choice for a reading activity (Ivey & Broaddus, 2001). Also similar to read alouds, independent reading offers students tremendous literacy benefits. Just 20 minutes of daily reading may provide as many as 1,000 new words in a student's working vocabulary (Nagy et al., 1987). Despite the inarguable benefits of independent reading and students' clear desire for it to be included in the instructional day, it remains conspicuously absent in instructional planning and scheduling (Allington, 2013).

So, how can you take advantage of this underused powerhouse for increasing student engagement and literacy skills, and where can you integrate it within the instructional day? There are a number of possibilities—at the beginning of the school day, between classes when there is a bit of unscheduled time, after lunch, or right before the end the day. It is your choice, but this kernel of time will provide extensive dividends in students' literacy growth and development.

When you have found time for it in your schedule, your next task is to determine what your independent program will look like in your classroom. Independent reading programs take a number of different approaches. Some focus on free reading experiences, while other demand students apply and document their use of reading strategies; still others compel students to record amounts read and summaries of the text. Below are some basic recommendations:

1. *Analyze the needs of your students, and identify what approach your independent program will take.* Determine how much guidance your students will need and to what degree you want your students to apply literacy skills from the literacy block. We recommend that at the very least you task students with recording what they read each day with a brief summary (i.e., one or two sentences) of the text.

2. *Model the importance of independent reading and your personal commitment.* If students are to view reading as an enjoyable activity, they need to see teachers reading alongside them. Equally important, however, is to leverage this time as a means to share your personal pleasure in books through weekly 3- to 5-minute book talks about texts that you are reading that they may also enjoy. In time, encourage students to lead brief book talks about texts they would recommend. Additionally, scheduling brief individual conferences to talk about books can be incredibly powerful. This allows you to talk about reading at a more evaluative level as well as to ensure that students are indeed making meaning of the text and grasping its ideas. Despite the fact that Hunt, as the father of silent sustained reading, might be assumed to assert that independent reading should be solitary, he actually voiced the belief that teacher-student conferences and book talks were at the heart of silent reading time.

3. *Supply a range of reading materials.* Experts often recommend that classroom libraries contain at least 10 books per child or approximately 300 books with a variety of text types and levels. We also find that students enjoy the prospect of a "field trip" to the school library. In addition to making it a special time for book selection, students observe the practice of going to the library as a natural part of one's day so that it becomes habituated in their own lives.

4. *Encourage engagement.* A large hurdle will be the student who says, "I hate reading!" To us, this is the greatest

challenge and the most exciting opportunity to make a difference in students' lives. For those students who utter these words—whether quietly with their heads dropped down or loudly so that everyone in the class knows exactly how much they dislike reading—we always respond with the same words: "You just haven't found your book yet. It's out there; we just have to find it!" We often find interest inventories and one-on-one interviews to produce the greatest trove of information about students. Discover what they're interested in . . . and you will find what they want to read.

5. *Build a system of accountability into the program.* Many programs lack accountability and without a sense of being held responsible, students may have their eyes on the text with their minds engaged elsewhere. A number of measures have proven effective to monitor student engagement, including reading logs, reader-response journals, writing text summaries, teacher-student book conferences and peer discussions. You decide the level of engagement you want to sustain, but accountability must be a key element.

Independent reading may take a bit of planning and maintaining, but it will soon become your students' favorite part of the day—as well as yours. Diana has often said that she always loved her independent reading time when she was playing a bit of jazz or classical music in the background and could look out over a sea of faces immersed in reading. For young students, second language learners or struggling readers, we also recommend audio books so that all students experiences the power of reading. However you design it, independent reading is that quiet time where everyone is reading for the sheer enjoyment of where books can take them.

Book Groups

In addition to teacher-led read alouds and the somewhat solitary practice of independent reading, book groups are effective as a vehicle to engage in authentic discourse about books. A number of experts maintain that social interaction is a valuable aspect of independent reading programs (Garan & DeVoogd, 2008; Reutzel, Jones, & Newman, 2010) as would be expected as we know that literacy acquisition is substantially a social process by which students learn from you as well as each other.

To participate in a book group, students must read the same text. Essential for a discussion, it also provides students reading buddies, comprehension support, and a motivating reason to read. In this context, students may read independently or with classmates and then meet with their book group once a week to talk about what they are reading. Alternatively, students may read the entirety of the book together, discussing as they go. In either case, book groups allow students to approach reading much as adults do—as an opportunity to interact socially and consider the text at a more interpretive and evaluative level than when reading alone.

Book groups provide the capstone experience of all the extended reading opportunities provided throughout the academic day. Read alouds are teacher directed and present the most instructional support, while independent reading compels students to take more responsibility for their own learning. Only when moving to book groups, however, are students expected to be autonomous and approach reading in a manner more reminiscent of an adult than a child. Taken together, these experiences offer a scaffolded approach for students to apply the skills and strategies taught during the literacy block in more authentic, real-world contexts.

Extended Reading Opportunities "In Action"

As a fifth-grade teacher, Ms. Evans worries about her students not reading. While her students have the skills and continue to show improvement during literacy block instruction, they are apathetic about reading for enjoyment. She is beginning to consider the ways she could encourage her students to read beyond the expected times with her.

First, she decided to re-design her read alouds. Although she had always read aloud to her students, she began to select an array of texts that she thought would appeal to a broad range of her class, such as information books that enriched what they were learning in science and social studies, newspaper articles about current events, movie reviews, song lyrics, poems, and stories from a mix of genres and cultures. She even made time to talk to the art and music teacher to find out what students were learning in those classes. On one occasion, before embarking on a new art project about origami, Ms. Evans read a book about the art of Japanese origami. Eventually, she began to take requests. Every other week, students could ask her for a particular article, book, or topic that they would like to hear. Throughout all of these read alouds, however, Ms. Evans always made sure that she asked students questions periodically to ensure their understanding, scaffolding their discussion from literal comprehension to more inferential points about the text as well as to an evaluative stance. In effect, she wanted her students not only to understand the text at a deeper level but also to assess both the quality of the text as well as their opinion about it.

Ms. Evans realized that although the read alouds were becoming a success both instructionally and for the enjoyment of her students, she needed them to see reading as something they did on their own as well. Her first problem was scheduling. Her day was already brimming over without a lot of time left for anything else. After looking carefully, she discovered that she had a bit of time at the start of the day. She decided that while she marked down her roll and took care of the "beginning-of-the-day tasks," students could use that time to read.

To get her students started, she requested a visit to the school library. Working with the school librarian, they helped every student select a book. She explained to her students, however, that they could also read something from outside the school collection, such as their own magazines, graphic novels, electronic readers, or web-based reading. The only condition was that the reading had to appropriate for reading in school. Armed with all of their texts, she explained to students that they would have 20 minutes every day just to read. The next day when students entered the classroom, they were greeted with instrumental music playing softly in the background. Ms. Evans asked them all to take their seats and begin reading. After she completed her work, she took out a book and began to read with them. They continued this way for several days, and then she gave each student a daily reading log and asked them to jot down what they were reading and a brief summary of the text.

Most students seemed to enjoy this quiet way to begin the day and were soon engrossed in their reading. Others changed their selections frequently and appeared to lose interest quickly. To work with them, Ms. Evans began to set up reading conferences with these students and asked them why they were struggling to settle on a text to read, what sort of things they were interested in, what genres they favored, what they had read in the past that they had enjoyed, etc. Some students, with her help, became increasingly more engaged. Others still bounced from text to text as she continued to counsel them. For these students, she brought a variety of text types until she could discover the reading "niche" to which they responded. In addition, she conferenced with students about the texts themselves—why did they choose the text, what was happening in it, what big ideas were they taking away from the author, would they recommend the book to someone else, etc.

Ms. Evans also began to offer weekly book talks. She tried to highlight a wide range of texts—some with which her students were familiar and some that would offer new experiences. Making them as interesting as possible to spark their interest, she made certain that the texts she highlighted were available in her class for students to check out. Soon, she began to have a waiting list as students gravitated toward her book talk selections. Building off their popularity, she invited her class to lead book talks as well, and students shared about texts that they were reading. Ms. Evans began to see a community of readers emerging from her class. The next step was for them to view reading as a social event and not something they did solely by themselves.

She first introduced the idea of book groups when her class began a genre study during the literacy block. As students naturally gravitated to certain genres, e.g., mysteries, historical fiction, information, poetry, she asked them to sign up for book groups. They could read together or alone. They could talk daily or read only. The only non-negotiable was that once a week they had to talk with their book group about the text they were all reading. Ms. Evans prepared some general questions as a starting point, but students could discuss any aspect of the text they liked. As she moved unobtrusively from group to group, she heard a variety of conversations. Some centered more heavily on the literal events of the text. Others seemed to be looking at the bigger picture of what the author was trying to communicate through the text; while still others seemed to take on the role of book critics, evaluating the author's writing style, the way the story developed or the information was presented, and considering if they would read anything else from that author. As students experienced success with book clubs, she looked for ways to incorporate them into her day and eventually decided to offer book clubs at least once a quarter, presenting students choice between reading independently with personal choice and book clubs with shared reading opportunities. Gradually, the 20 minutes a day that Ms. Evans had found became one of the most important and most enjoyable parts of her school day. Students were actually reading, finding what texts engaged them, learning from the reading practices of others, and coming to view reading not as a subject to be learned but as a part of their normal lives.

Ms. Evans slowly integrated read alouds, independent reading, and book groups into her instructional day. Although she had to overcome the hurdles of scheduling and student engagement, these opportunities for expanded reading became a mainstay in her classroom. She also found that students' reading proficiency increased as well as their natural enjoyment in reading itself. Looking back, her students had grown substantially, and a great deal of that growth stemmed from the careful planning and delivery of the everyday read aloud and 20 minutes of found time for students to read merely for the sake of reading.

Conclusion

Too often the literacy block is the sole reading experience that students find in schools. Rather than an arduous task, offering expanded reading opportunities encourage students to view reading as a form of recreation—whether it be to find information on the Internet, read a movie review, find a great story, or just read the lyrics of a favorite song—that is simply part of their normal day. Simply put, it is not just about teaching students how to read; it is about teaching them to become readers.

Read alouds, independent reading programs, and book groups constitute the backbone of reading outside the literacy block. With intentional planning and careful implementation, they present students with motivational reasons to read and change the way they view literacy in their lives. With this much power to influence student perspectives on reading, they cannot be a luxury . . . they must become an integral part of the instructional day.

Part III

Ensuring Student Success

- Differentiating Instruction
- Project-Based Learning
- Assessment

8

Differentiating Instruction

As we contemplated what to title this book, we carefully considered each word and its implications for teaching and learning. We purposefully selected the terms *re-envisioning the literacy block* and *maximizing instruction* because we wanted you, as an educator, to change your paradigm of how you define the literacy block and what it can achieve in your students' lives. One inarguable means to ensure a changed outlook on literacy instruction is the inclusion of systematic differentiation, which is widely acknowledged as a hallmark of maximizing instruction for all students. Similarly important is the awareness that differentiation cannot be secured through a commercial program or a single strategy; rather, differentiation is a philosophy that guides the decisions that you make every day to ensure that you are meeting students where they are and scaffolding their learning through a personal pathway to reach their greatest potential.

> "Schools cannot equalize children; schools can only equalize opportunity."
> *(Hollingworth, 1922, p. 29)*

Differentiation in some form takes place in every classroom, but the tactics we take are important. For example, Carol Ann Tomlinson, a pioneer in the field of differentiation, cautions that we often separate students based on their abilities and then alter how we teach each of the groups according to our expectations of their skills. Tomlinson (2009) argues that "a foundational principle of differentiation is 'teaching up'—that is, developing the kind of rich, authentic curriculum we often restrict to our most able learners, then differentiating instruction to lift the majority of students to success with these goals" (p. 30).

How important is differentiation? In diverse classrooms where no differentiated practices are in place, the achievement of average and low-achieving students is diminished and high-achieving students make only moderate gains (McGill-Franzen, Zmach, Solic, & Zeig, 2006); conversely, in classrooms where differentiation is carried out, academic increases are documented for students from all ranges of the achievement spectrum (Rock, Gregg, Ellis, & Gable, 2008), including students with mild or severe learning disabilities—especially when teaching is centered in small groups or with targeted instruction (McQuarrie, McRae, & Stack-Cutler, 2008). Students also demonstrate specific improvement in phonemic skills, decoding, and comprehension, as well as improved attitudes toward reading (Baumgartner, Lipowski, & Rush, 2003).

Recognizing the weight it carries for achievement, educators are often asked how they differentiate for their students within the literacy block. When posed with this question, they typically focus on their use of flexible grouping and guided reading. These are unquestionably components of differentiated instruction; however, they are empty promises if we do not have a solid understanding of literacy instruction and its developmental progression, recognize the specific strengths and weaknesses of our students, and know what to do instructionally with students once we have them in these settings. For example, educators who place students in lower-achieving groups often provide less exposure to text, while students placed in higher-achieving groups are given richer experiences with text at a quicker rate, which perpetuates the Matthew Effect—the rich get richer and the poor get poorer. Consequently, students who struggle are actually held back by their reduced experiences, while those who achieve continue to be challenged and enhance their literacy skills, thus widening the achievement gap. True differentiation, Ankrum and Bean (2008) argue, "means that the lesson focus will be different for each group" (p. 144); yet, we must still strive to ensure that all students achieve grade-level curricular expectations through a shifting balance of remediation, scaffolding, and acceleration. Implementing differentiated instruction, however, can be problematic because it conjures up images of remediation for the struggling student. This is only one facet of this approach to teaching and learning. Differentiation is about modifying the educational experiences of all students through remediation—but also through scaffolding and acceleration. The one-size-fits-all approach simply does not meet the needs of the majority of learners in our classrooms. How do you determine which type of instruction is necessary? Teaching has to adhere to the concept of "readiness" in which instruction should be slightly beyond the student's current mastery level—a concept based on the Zone of Proximal Development and scaffolding—and an anchor of the Core Literacy Block. This notion of readiness should not be viewed as only a need of the young or the struggling learner; readiness has implications for all learners in determining whether at any given time of the instructional process they would benefit from remediation, scaffolding, or acceleration.

An often forgotten population in this equation is the high achiever. In our passionate determination to save our most vulnerable students, we sometimes forget about those who seemingly can achieve without us—the high-performing students who consistently score at the top of the class and appear quite capable of learning on their own. This belief has brought about some disturbing outcomes in the lives of those about whom we worry the least. One illustration of this is found in dropout statistics. Conventional wisdom suggests that students drop out of school because of academic deficits, but the dropout rate for gifted students is nearly identical to the dropout rate for non-gifted students, with approximately 20% of all dropouts identified as gifted (Cloud, 2007). Considering this rate of withdrawal, high-achieving students cannot be overlooked in their

134 ◆ Ensuring Student Success

needs for differentiated learning opportunities. In fact, Phillips (2008) makes the compelling argument that "the risk with prioritizing one group in today's burdened schools is that the needs of others are likely to be displaced" (p. 51).

Individualizing Instruction for Students

The most exemplary teachers use a variety of grouping practices—whole group, small group, and individualized instruction—to meet the needs of their class (Pressley et al., 2001) but teach most often in small groups with attention given to individual students. To offer prescriptive teaching and learning to small numbers of students, they use assessments to form flexible instructional groups, rearranging students based on their assessment results while continuing to expose lower-achieving groups to the same number of high-level teaching strategies as those in higher-achieving groups (Taylor, Pearson, Clark, & Walpole, 2000).

Systematic, ongoing assessment, then, plays a pivotal role in an educator's ability to inform high-quality individualized instruction. While formal assessment is one consideration, you should also include formative assessments, anecdotal records, and observational notes to develop comprehensive insight into your students' competencies. Begin with learning profiles (e.g., academic performance records, learning preferences, hobbies, literacy attitudes) to organize students into common groups. Then, continue formative assessment throughout your instruction to help you orchestrate and sustain an individualized learning plan for each student (Heacox, 2009) as well as suggest avenues for differentiated practices in your classroom.

Designing a classroom devoted to systematic differentiated practices can be daunting. The Core Literacy Block, however, is based on essential elements of differentiation, such as flexible grouping, scaffolding, varied instructional materials, individualized vocabulary study, small-group study and collaboration, prescriptive strategy instruction, leveled questioning, etc. In addition to these underpinnings of differentiation, however, you can also augment your ability to individualize instruction through three strategic modes.

When considering ways to differentiate learning experiences for students, we typically consider the three components of content, process, and product (Tomlinson, 1999). Content is *what* we teach; it is our curriculum. We can modify it by the texts we select, the resources we provide, and the choices we offer. Process refers to *how* we teach and *how* students learn. It addresses the uniqueness of students—their abilities, their preferences for learning, and their interests—and can be adapted by the complexity and rigor of the tasks and the manner in which students can learn the content. Product deals with the way in which students demonstrate their learning. It transforms assessment from the one-size-fits-all to a range of options that extend beyond the paper-and-pencil format. Let's take a look at each of these components and how they can transform literacy instruction.

Content

Differentiating content refers to tailoring what students learn or how they will access the learning in order to gain the requisite knowledge and skills. These modifications can take place through a number of different avenues, including grouping strategies, the use of vocabulary study at specified readiness levels and not based solely on grade-level placements of students, varied instructional materials, selection of appropriate content based on student assessment, etc. Below are some examples that have powerful effects on teaching and learning.

At the core of differentiated practices lies flexible grouping. When you group your class and create targeted activities prescriptive to the learning needs of the individual groups, you have implemented flexible instructional grouping (Heacox, 2002). This strategy is a customary feature of the literacy block; unfortunately, too often our groups are not flexible but actually restrict students into the same configurations throughout the course of the academic year. If flexible grouping is to be effective, the composition of groups should be fluid as students move in and out based on their strengths and needs in relation to a specific learning objective.

Another technique to differentiate content is to offer a range of instructional texts at varied reading levels. Consider a class that is learning about author's purpose. While all students need to acquire this concept, the texts to teach them about it differ. Groups can and should be reading assorted texts that align to their current reading competencies. So, while the learning objective remains the same, the manner in which students access that content varies.

As we said earlier in this chapter, we must never lose sight of our students who excel. Typical issues that hinder our support of these children are a lack of training to meet these specialized needs along with a shortage of appropriate enrichment materials (Stamps, 2004). While these concerns may seem overwhelming among all of the other challenges of today's classroom, Sally Reis, an expert in gifted education, argues that "this lack of curriculum modification may be the single largest reason for under-achievement in this population" (Kirschenbaum, 1995, p. 24). Indeed, "the recurring message from research is that it is the teacher, not the programs or materials that makes the difference; therefore, only a well-prepared teacher can effectively differentiate reading instruction for students" (Ankrum & Bean, 2008, p. 143).

Colangelo and colleagues (2004) conducted a meta-analysis of studies from 1932–1991, a review of 380 individual studies, and an examination of four longitudinal studies extending 10 and 20 years—from which they determined the undeniable benefits of curriculum acceleration for motivated and capable learners, and curriculum compacting is one of the most commonly used acceleration approaches. "The purpose of curriculum compacting as an instructional strategy is to provide high ability students with enrichment opportunities over and above the regular school curriculum" (Stamps, 2004, p. 33). What should be guaranteed is that high-achieving students not be given more of the same study that they have already mastered—not additional worksheets, not more questions to answer, or not devoting their instructional time tutoring peers who need additional support—nor should it be assumed that curriculum compacting is only effective with upper-grade students. Rather, curriculum compacting has the ability to support students as early as first grade (Stamps, 2004).

What is curriculum compacting? It is a strategy developed to ensure high-achieving students maximize their time for learning. In Phase 1, the focus is on "defining the goals and outcomes of a given unit or segment of instruction." The goal here is to analyze the content to be taught to the class as a whole. During Phase 2, the teacher is "identifying students who have already mastered the objectives or outcomes of a unit that is about to be taught" and then assessing them on the content to ensure their proficiency of the content. If students miss a couple of questions on this pre-assessment, the teacher looks for trends and then supplies targeted learning materials just for that small deficit. For the onset of Phase 3, the teacher concentrates on "providing acceleration and enrichment options" and prepares alternative learning experiences, such as self-directed learning activities, hands-on research projects, investigations, and self-selected mini-courses. In this way, students move along their own personalized learning pathway—not waste their learning time on content they have already mastered. Used as a means to motivate, curriculum compacting has also been found to drive under-performing students to complete regular classroom assignments in order to "earn time" for their own self-selected units of study (Reis & Renzulli, 1992).

Process

Process relates to how students make sense of the content and how educators provide diverse experiences for their learning. While there is a myriad of strategies to differentiate process, we will focus on just one—questioning. We are emphasizing questioning because it has the greatest potential to increase academic rigor and student performance.

The importance of academic discourse derives from the instructional principle that the type of talk patterns found in classrooms shape the thinking produced by students, and "to a great extent within classrooms, the language used by teachers and students determines what is learned and how learning takes place" (Wilkinson & Silliman, 2000, p. 337), echoing the long-recognized embedded role discussion maintains in student learning (Beck, McKeown, Hamilton, & Kucan, 1997; Cazden, John, & Hymes, 1972; Hoetker & Ahlbrand, 1969; Palincsar & Brown, 1989; Vygotsky, 1978).

In considering the parameters of academic discourse, Durkin's 1978/1979 seminal study revealed that questioning is by far the most common classroom activity with 18% of instructional time devoted to teacher-posed questions. A subsequent study by Leven and Long (1981) determined that teachers ask approximately 300–400 questions a day. With 180 school days in an average academic year, teachers potentially pose 72,000 questions annually. Over the entirety of a K–12 educational experience that number reaches 936,000 questions, indicating nearly 1,000,000 opportunities to engage students in critical thinking and reflective analysis of content.

Despite the academic potential of questioning, the marginalization of talk as a means for students to process content, to organize their understanding of information, and to communicate their thinking has persisted in classrooms. This can be illustrated through the prevailing presence of the two-thirds rule, which states that two-thirds of classroom time is devoted to talking, two-thirds of the talking is dominated by teachers, and two-thirds of teacher talk is directed (Flanders, 1970), such as is found in the traditional question-answer discourse pattern commonly referred to as Initiation-Response-Evaluation, or IRE, in which the teacher poses a question to which he or she already knows the answer as a means to ascertain if students have learned the material, a student responds briefly, and then the teacher evaluates the quality of the answer, offering brief responses like "Yes," "Good answer," or "No, that is not correct."

Also identified as the recitation method, once completed, the process begins again with a new question, and the pattern continues (Cazden, 1988). In this three-part discourse pattern, teachers dominate the conversation, and students commonly respond in single words or phrases with pre-determined answers that leave little time for reflection or collaboration. Rather than utilizing classroom discussion as a means only to assess student learning, Kühnen and colleagues (2012) argue that "communication is an essential part of the learning processes itself, which is to say that students learn *by* communicating (and do not engage in communication only *after* they have achieved mastery over the learning material)" (p. 60).

The process of learning, then, should be modified through adjusting questions and activities to reflect higher-level thinking appropriate to the needs of the students. Rather than posing the same questions to all students, or more importantly the same level of cognitive rigor, questions should be differentiated based on the skill set of the students being asked—while remembering to scaffold student thinking to advance their thinking.

Differentiated questions can easily be crafted if you base them on a standardized metric, e.g., Bloom's Taxonomy, Webb's Depth of Knowledge (DOK) Levels, or the three levels of reading comprehension (i.e., literal, inferential, and evaluative). How does it work? Figure 8.1 uses Bloom's Taxonomy (Bloom, 1956) to design six different questions, all focusing on the fairy tale *Little Red Riding Hood*, at increasing levels of complexity. While this story is commonly found in the primary grades, notice how the questions pertaining to this simple tale vary widely in cognitive rigor and critical thinking.

In this example, all of the students may be reading a common text, but the questions differ widely based on their understanding of the text itself as well as their ability to think deeply about what they read. Importantly, while questions should be leveled, remember to scaffold questions just as you do with activities so that students are constantly stretched to think more rigorously. For example, you may have students who function more comfortably in the Knowledge level, but you will still drive them to reach toward the Comprehension level and beyond so that they continue to grow and develop.

The next example utilizes Webb's DOK Levels (Webb, 1997; 1999) using the same story but concentrating on the main character. Webb's DOK levels are grounded in cognitive rigor and can be used with questions, such as below, but also to categorize

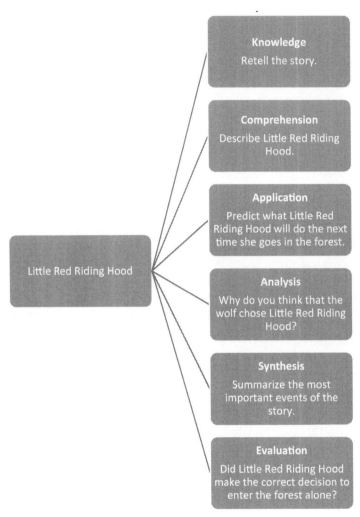

FIGURE 8.1 Leveling Question Complexity through Bloom's Taxonomy

instruction, learning activities, and assessments. In this model, there are four levels. Level 1, Recall and Reproduction, necessitates students only to lift information directly from the text with no inferencing or critical thinking needed. In Level 2, Skills and Concepts, the learner must now move beyond the words on the page to draw conclusions about the text. Level 3, Strategic Thinking, compels students to problem solve and rationalize their thought process. In fact, it is the need to explain their

Differentiating Instruction ♦ 141

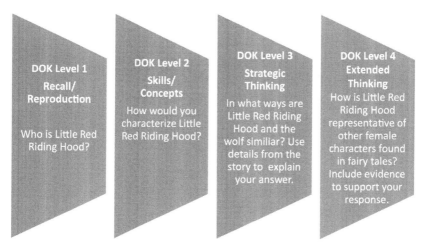

FIGURE 8.2 Leveling Question Complexity through Webb's DOK Levels

reasoning and cite evidence that is the primary attribute of Level 3. Finally in Level 4, Extended Thinking, students synthesize their understanding and evaluate what they have learned in multiple contexts. In Figure 8.2, we focus our questions on just characterization.

For another leveling system, Figure 8.3 illustrates the levels, or layers, of reading comprehension, using the story of *Little Red Riding Hood* to focus on setting. This model encompasses literal, inferential, and evaluative understanding, and

> although literal comprehension is undoubtedly important (without surface-level understanding of a text, deeper interactions with the text are not possible) . . . literal understanding is a stepping-stone to more advanced comprehension skills that must also be examined to continue to see growth in student performance. (Basaraba, Yovanoff, Alonzo, & Tindal, 2013, p. 353)

Here there are only three questions, then, but they represent a comprehensive deepening of student understanding of text.

Any of these models will assist you in leveling the questions you pose to students. To make certain that we encourage a broad

Literal	• Where does the story take place?
Inferential	• Why do you think Little Red Riding Hood stopped in the forest?
Evaluative	• How is the setting of the forest important to the story?

FIGURE 8.3 Leveling Question Complexity through the Three Levels of Reading Comprehension

range of thinking skills, we often select a model, like DOK, and then draft questions from each of the four tiers of cognitive rigor to guide whole-group discussion. That way we can raise the quality of our class talk and expose students to questions they may not ordinarily experience.

Product

Differentiating the product obliges you to adjust the ways in which students can demonstrate their mastery of content. This may take place through traditional tests, varied writing tasks, artwork, song, dance, technology, etc. It may also be a matter of changing the product so that students are familiar with a range of assessments. Tomlinson (2001) suggests that

> many students can show what they know far better in a product than on a written test. Therefore, in a differentiated classroom, teachers may replace some tests with rich product assignments, or combine tests and product options so the broadest range of students has maximum opportunity to think about, apply, and demonstrate what they have learned. (p. 85)

Whatever form the product takes, it is important to develop guidelines and rubrics prior to beginning so that students have a clear understanding of expectations and demonstrate their learning in the best possible way. (See Chapter 10 for more information on assessment.)

Conclusion

Differentiation is critical as "teachers who employ differentiated instruction adjust their teaching for students of differing abilities . . . with the intent of maximizing each student's growth and individual success by meeting each student where he or she is and assisting in the learning process" (Dixon, Yssel, McConnell, & Hardin, 2014, p. 113). Differentiating, through content, process, or product, allows learning to take place so that all of our students reach their potential. One-size-fits-all is not an option. Your students deserve learning experiences designed to ensure their success, and differentiation helps makes that goal a reality.

9

Project-Based Learning

Disengaged . . . unmotivated . . . apathetic. These disheartening descriptors are increasingly employed as students mature. Some students enter our classrooms excited to learn. Sadly, others do not. Attitudes toward reading, writing, and school at large systematically decline as students progress through the grades, perhaps in part because little opportunity is given to them to explore their personal interests or have choices in their own learning. Instead, we plan lessons about which our students may not see the relevance to their own lives.

As educators continue to strive toward strengthening literacy skills and ensuring that students are prepared for the demands of this new century, concerns have been raised for greater focus on 21st century skills. While the imperative of the 3Rs—reading, 'riting, and 'rithmetic—is indisputable and must remain at the core of teaching and learning, the 4Cs of the 21st century classroom—communication, collaboration, critical thinking, and creative thinking—cannot be ignored. Students must be expected, and taught how, to share their thoughts and ideas with others, to work as a team to achieve a goal, and to think more deeply

> "PBL [Project-Based Learning] is the best teaching practice for the new millennium."
> *(Bender, 2012, p. 182)*

and innovatively about the work that they complete. Of these four components, it is critical thinking, however, that tends to be the most challenging to nurture within our students as it is not a skill or concept to be easily instructed upon or assessed. Rather, it demands something much more nebulous and harder to attain.

> Because critical thinking is a mental habit that requires students to think about their thinking and about improving the process, it requires students to use higher-order thinking skills—not memorize data or accept what they read or are told without critically thinking. . . . Traditional instructional methods use too many facts and not enough conceptualization; too much memorizing and not enough thinking. Therefore, lecture and rote memorization do not promote critical thinking. (Snyder & Snyder, 2008, pp. 91–92)

While the literacy block we envision rejects rote processes of learning, more must be done to ensure that students become independent readers, writers, and thinkers. How can you infuse 21st century skills into your classroom in addition to the core instruction of the literacy block we have described thus far? One powerful method is the addition of project-based learning.

What Is Project-Based Learning?

William H. Kirkpatrick discussed project-based learning in the United States as early as 1918 but referred to it as the Project Method and described it as a "hearty, purposeful act" taken on by students. The importance of "purpose" within the project's design can be seen in the educational view for which Kirkpatrick is most closely known—"We learn what we live." He believed that the learning process was augmented by using literacy in authentic, real-world contexts encompassing interdisciplinary study that he asserted would strengthen background knowledge as well as, ultimately, improve academic performance. This conviction in the significance of learning by doing was carried on by Dewey who emphasized the value of experiential learning—all of which is grounded in constructivist learning often associated with the work of Vygotsky.

Project-based learning (PBL) consists of a systematic approach to teaching that is initiated with a driving question posed to students through which they engage in a sustained, student-led, real-world investigation with a culminating product or presentation that has meaning and purpose outside of the classroom. Common projects revolve around a number of inquiry scenarios: a search for the solution to a problem, an examination of a philosophical question, an inquiry into a controversial issue, a search into a historical event or person, an analysis of a scientific phenomenon, or a design of a model or concept. It captivates the natural curiosity of children and gives them an authentic need to read while simultaneously ensuring a level of autonomy and responsibility not typically found in the traditional instructional day. While the duration of projects is flexible to the demands of the project goals as well as student need, they most commonly continue for 2 to 4 weeks. PBL should necessitate reading and writing as well as speaking and listening with students presenting their learning to public audiences as a capstone experience of the project.

Figure 9.1 illustrates the key characteristics of PBL, such as projects begin with a compelling, open-ended question that drives the inquiry in which students will engage. That question should be rooted in a real-life exploration, stirring the curiosity of students and eliciting interest in finding the answer to the question presented. It should also be embedded in the curriculum so the PBL project supports the school's learning goals and makes curriculum come alive in the world outside the classroom. These realistic investigations are carefully planned for and prepared by the educator, but it should also oblige students to take responsibility for their own learning as they work collaboratively to

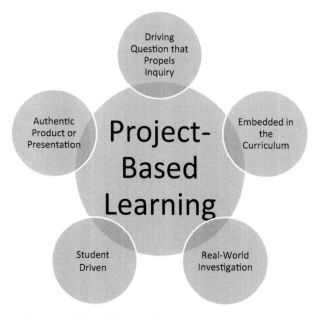

FIGURE 9.1 Characteristics of Project-Based Learning

approach the question (e.g., collaboration, research strategies, problem solving) and later to present their answer (e.g., presentations, reports, brochures, posters).

The Power of Project-Based Learning

Research has consistently found that PBL projects deliver a number of positive benefits to student learning. For example, they are well known for their ability to increase student engagement and motivation (Bell, 2010). Academically, students who participate in PBL improve their critical reasoning and problem-solving skills (Licht, 2014; Mergendoller, Maxwell, & Bellisimo, 2006) as well as show evidence of increased gains in content knowledge over that of students taught with more traditional methods (Kaldi, Fillipatou, & Govaris, 2011). Likewise, they perform better on standardized assessments (Alacapinar, 2008). These benefits extend to struggling students as documented in one study when the researcher noted that "their motivation to learn, their discipline and their willingness to work on their projects longer hours indicate that they behaved like high achievers" (Doppelt, 2003, p. 264).

Misconceptions about Project-Based Learning

Although PBL has recognized benefits and a history of support by educational theorists and researchers, it is not a common aspect of classroom practice. A key confusion that triggers such disregard is the mistaken belief that PBL produces teaching and learning that is contrary to the systematic instruction that the school typically provides. Educators in the field often question how a traditional literacy block model can function in tandem with project-based learning. It becomes a contention between two separate and opposing pedagogical philosophies. Either you follow the conventional teacher-directed literacy block, or you foster the practices of student-driven project-based learning. Can one actually exist with the other? The answer is a resounding—yes!

> Students not only need to know how to use a skill but also when to use it. They need to learn to recognize for themselves the contexts in which the skill might be useful and the purposes it can most appropriately serve. Project work and systematic instruction can be seen as providing complementary learning opportunities. In systematic instruction, the students acquire the skills, and in project work, they apply those skills in meaningful contexts. Project work can thus be seen as the part of the curriculum planned in negotiation with the students and supportive of (and extending) the more formal and teacher-directed instructional elements. (Systematic Instruction and the Project Approach, n.d.)

PBL projects actually consolidate the effects of the literacy block. In fact, as we re-envision the literacy block, PBL projects provide a greater extension of the gradual release of responsibility model. Students develop their literacy skills with our scaffolded, guided support and then convert their learning into applications in the real world. What better way is there to demonstrate to students that what we teach them in the literacy block will benefit them personally and in the world around them?

Another common misconception is that all projects are synonymous with project-based learning. They are not. Traditional projects are teacher directed with pre-determined activities and focus on a specific, teacher-selected product that students must submit. PBL is student driven and emphasizes the learning and mental habits generated throughout the process—not just a culminating product.

A further distinction is that these teacher-planned activities propel projects into a linear pathway. Conversely, PBL projects are more personally led by students and thus move through a multitude of different pathways to arrive at an answer, naturally producing unanticipated student actions and richer, more authentic learning.

Educators also believe that while projects strive to be engaging and motivating for students, they lack academic rigor and alignment to academic standards. This cannot be further from the reality of a carefully planned PBL project. At the very initiation, the driving question should derive from academic standards, and the work that students complete should be assessed through the lens of the expectations of those same standards.

A further concern is that they are appropriate only for older students, yet PBL projects can be highly significant for the intellectual growth of young children as young as 4 and 5 years of age as they build interconnected knowledge of the world around them (Yuen, 2009). Catherwood (1999) argues that "experiences that support the child in making connections amongst domains of knowledge experiences . . . are likely to impact on and enhance the richness of the neural networks in the child's brain" (p. 33).

Even with misconceptions resolved, PBL is not easily implemented. Many impediments exist that must be overcome. Let's look at the most prevalent and how we can eliminate them.

Obstacles in Implementing Project-Based Learning

A number of barriers exist in the implementation of PBL, such as the time involved, resources, balancing content areas equitably, curricular demands, and professional expertise to design and manage projects. The most common hurdle, however, is the paradigm of traditional, teacher-centered teaching versus student-centered inquiry. To implement PBL, you must be willing to surrender the locus of control from one of you as the expert in the classroom to you as a facilitator for your students in their role of learners and investigators.

Figure 9.2 highlights some of the differences betwen traditional teaching and the more student-centered PBL. In the traditional teaching model, educators remain the experts in the classrooms to whom students go to learn. As such, there is typically a single source of learning—be it the teacher or the textbook. Students tend to complete work centered on school-based

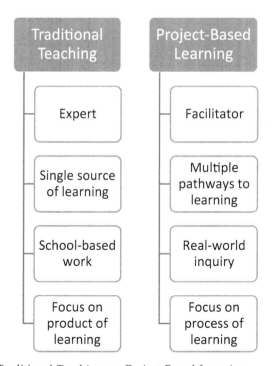

FIGURE 9.2 Traditional Teaching vs. Project-Based Learning

outcomes with a predetermined product that all students must accomplish. In contrast, PBL emphasizes the teacher as a facilitator for students in which they are viewed as independent readers, writers, and thinkers that approach learning with the understanding that there are multiple pathways they may and will take in order to conduct an investigation of a real-world problem. Their investigation, in effect, is more important than whatever product they create as they learn more about themselves and the world beyond their classroom walls by the process they take to acquire this new learning.

Integration of Projects into the Literacy Block

Project-based learning can be integrated within literacy instruction in a number of ways. Hallermann, Larger, and Mergendoller (2011) suggest that PBL operates upon a spectrum with varying degrees of integration within daily classroom instruction. It may function as a completely separate entity from the literacy block and its focus on reading and writing development. In this approach, projects are completed outside of the literacy block, typically in the content area study of social studies, science, or math—with no genuine link to literacy instruction. Partial implementation of PBL combines all of the content areas, including literacy, at least to some degree. In this model, the teacher designs a focus that will directly support the work of students in their projects. At the highest level, full implementation of PBL offers the most complete integration of content study—with literacy as an anchor to student inquiry. Here, the project becomes the method of learning content, and literacy is actually learned through the project itself. The instructional time for this implementation may be found in the content area study, or it may be established during the literacy block itself. In this contingency, for the brief period of the PBL project, the literacy block—as it is typically approached—is re-envisioned while students conduct their PBL investigation. For example, rather than following the whole group, guided reading, and small-group work model, the teacher holds a whole-group meeting both to launch the project and to provide a time for students to share their progress for teacher monitoring and support. The remainder of the time is devoted to students' independent research, collaboration, and preparation for how they will present their findings. This appropriation of time may seem the most aggressive and paradigm-shifting, but it also communicates to students that the application of their literacy skills in real-world investigations are as important as the more traditional instruction in which they typically participate.

Teachers make use of PBL in a variety of ways. Those who utilize projects as *initiators* to more traditional study provide research questions to guide student inquiry with a culminating product that naturally leads to the launch of a new unit of study. Some employ the projects as a *reinforcer* to supplement content already completed through more traditional teaching methods. Others leverage them as *extenders* of the curriculum for opportunities to think more critically and problem solve about their learning. It is important to understand, however, that there is no "best" way to employ PBL projects in the classroom. Those who rely on projects as *navigators* are cognizant of this and select the form that best suits the needs of the curriculum as well as the needs of the students (Tamin & Grant, 2013).

However you opt to bring about PBL projects, Larmer and Mergendoller (2010) suggest that there are seven essentials that should guide the planning and implementation into your classroom.

1. Capture students' interest through an "entry event," which can be anything relevant to the topic to be investigated, for example, a video clip, a guest speaker, a field trip, etc.
2. Initiate the project through a driving question that should encapsulate the focus of the project, be open-ended, and be directly linked to the academic concepts to be learned.
3. Give students voice and choice both in the way they engage with the investigation as well as how they present their findings.
4. Emphasize 21st century skills, like collaboration, critical thinking, and technology use.

154 ◆ Ensuring Student Success

5. Use inquiry and innovation to guide students through multiple pathways in the search for knowledge.
6. Ensure feedback and revision so that students are supported in their work as well as understand that high-quality products require effort and ongoing improvement.
7. Expect students to offer a publicly presented product.

Many practitioners of PBL also suggest that the most efficient way to design a project is to start with the end in mind. Using a backward design, you can determine what you want your students to learn and what educational outcomes you hope to achieve. Consider the scenario of a second-grade classroom focusing on the characteristics of folktales—an expectation stemming from the grade-level standard. How would you begin? First, design a driving question that will engage students in an investigation of some aspect of the world in which they live, such as "Are folktales from different parts of the world similar to our folktales?" Additionally, prepare appropriate resources that will be necessary for students to research their projects (e.g., expert visits, field trips, electronic media, web-based materials, books) and determine how students will warehouse their research and document their progress. For this particular unit, you would need to ensure that students had adequate access to a variety of folktales in print form as well as on film. As a means of organization, students may work collaboratively in groups investigating various regions of the world, that is, Europe, Asia, and Africa. Reading different samples of folktales, students would note what elements of the stories they all share and document that in their research notebooks. Next, you would determine how the project will be assessed. Culminating products serve as a capstone of the PBL project and can be assessed in any number of ways—self-assessments, peer assessments, oral presentations, formal reports, student portfolios. The key to this final piece of the PBL project is to assess student learning in a way that is the most authentic to the driving question and the students' answer to that question. For students not experienced in PBL or for those in the primary grades, students may initially select from a menu of options and then with subsequent PBL projects begin to determine for themselves what product best represents their learning and the answer to their project's driving question. In the case of the folktale project, because the students are still at primary level, the teacher may decide to provide more guidance in how they will demonstrate their learning. One culminating activity may be the creation of a student-written folktale that encapsulates the primary characteristics of a folktale followed later by a presentation of it in play form.

Suggested PBL Study Topics

PBL projects should always be embedded into the curriculum—not as an additional unit of study unrelated to classroom study. Below is a potential list of PBL projects across grade levels and content areas. You may find them helpful if they correlate to your own instruction or, at the very least, as examples of potential study topics. While we have, somewhat artificially, delineated them within one particular content area, they are actually interdisciplinary and require skills across a range of academic contents.

Conclusion

Project-based learning offers an authentic application of the skills students acquire in the literacy block. In addition to being a motivating factor to engage students and supporting the academic standards put in place both for literacy as well as other interdisciplinary areas of study, Doppelt (2003) makes the case that

> In the future, children must enter a workforce in which they will be judged on their performance. They will be evaluated not only on their outcomes, but also on their collaborative, negotiating, planning, and organizational

TABLE 9.1 Sample PBL Study Topics

Grade	Literacy	Math	Social Studies	Science
Kindergarten	**Literature** "Describe what makes a good story."	**Shapes** "Where can I find shapes in the world around me?"	**Community Helpers** "What are important jobs in our community?"	**Animal Habitats** "Why do animals choose to live in the places that they do?"
1	**Fairy Tales** "What makes a story a fairy tale?"	**School Map** "Can you create a realistic map of your school in preparation for the arrival of a new student?"	**Holidays** "How do people from around the world celebrate holidays?"	**Five Senses** "How do we use our senses to understand the world around us?"
2	**Folktales** "Do folktales from different parts of the world share similar characteristics?"	**Money** "How do businesses make money?"	**Community** "You are the mayor of your city. What five things would you change and why?"	**Teeth** "How can we take care of our teeth?"
3	**Mythology** "What purpose do myths have, and do modern myths exist?"	**Personal Budget** "If you were given $100, how would you budget your money to get the most toys/ games/books?"	**National Monuments** "What is the importance of national monuments?"	**Water** "What if there were no more oceans?"
4	**Point of View** "How does point of view influence the reader's experience of a narrative?"	**Fractions** "How are fractions used in the kitchen?"	**Geography** "Why does geography matter?"	**Recycling** "How can we encourage students in our school to recycle?"

#				
5	**Genre Study** "How do stories from the same genre approach similar topics?"	**Video Games** "Does playing video games improve your math skills?"	**Natural Resources** "How does the availability of natural resources affect a nation's prosperity?"	**Nutrition** "Can you create a more nutritious menu for your favorite restaurant?"
6	**Accounts of Historical Events** "Are firsthand and secondhand accounts of historical events equally credible, and when can one be more important than the other?"	**Math/Art Connection** "How do artists use math?"	**Ancient Greece** "What would happen if ancient Greece had never developed the concept of democracy?"	**Climate** "How does climate influence the way we live?"
7	**Historical Fiction** "How does historical fiction shape the way we view history?"	**Rollercoaster** "Can you design a rollercoaster?"	**American History** "Was the Civil War inevitable?"	**Fossils** "What can we learn from a fossil?"
8	**Argumentative Writing** "Are elements of argumentative writing always used explicitly, or are they sometimes embedded in other writing genres? If so, why would a writer do this?"	**Financial Responsibility** "Can you plan a public relations campaign that would educate our community on the importance of financial responsibility?"	**Leadership in History** "What makes a good leader?"	**Infectious Diseases** "How can we stop the spread of flu in our homes, our communities, and our country?"

skills. By implementing PBL, we are preparing our students to meet the twenty-first century with preparedness and a repertoire of skills they can use successfully. (p. 43)

As we re-envision the literacy block, PBL offers another piece of the mosaic of how you can maximize instruction across all grade and performance levels to ensure that your students harness their innate curiosity to become self-reliant learners and thrive in this new technologically demanding world in which we all find ourselves.

10

Assessment

With the continuing scrutiny on standardized testing and its implications on how society views its significance in education, assessment has gained the reputation of being more important than instruction itself. It has, in some cases, become the sole barometer of what denotes an effective educator as if instruction itself has no bearing in the absence of "the test." While it is easy to be drawn into this assessment paradox, let's not forget that assessment exists only to support teaching and learning—not the other way around.

Assessment can only be truly effective if it directly aligns to your instruction. The first step is to determine what you consider essential that your students learn and realize that you assess what you value. Not sure about that? Think about what you currently assess; more than likely, you measure those competencies and skills that you deem important for your students to master. If you recognize this simple fact, then you just need to establish how and when you will assess—within an instructional lesson, at the conclusion of a unit, over the course of the academic year. Using assessment in this context allows you to create

160 ◆ Ensuring Student Success

> "The quality of instruction in any classroom turns on the quality of the assessments used there."
>
> *(Stiggins, 1999, p. 20)*

an assessment portfolio of your students' strengths, needs, and progress, and equally important, a guide for teaching and learning.

In many classrooms, educators continue to rely on traditional assessments, such as quizzes, end-of-chapter tests, and high-stakes, standardized assessments. That approach can be problematic because traditional assessment does not present a realistic portrait of a student's true academic abilities nor does it reflect acknowledged educational theories of how children learn. In addition, traditional assessment spotlights learning as a product rather than a process, with no attention to how the results can guide instruction. Of even greater concern is the current reality that dependence on standardized assessments has "undesirable effects on teaching and learning because they [lead] to a narrowing of the curriculum and an over-emphasis on basic skills" (Linn, 2000, p. 8).

What is also pivotal is that assessment is not just the measure that we use to judge students—but the measure that students use to judge themselves as well. Stiggins (2009) argues that

> those who see themselves succeeding early on begin to believe in themselves as able learners and behave accordingly. A self-fulfilling prophecy begins to play out that turns success into confidence, which gives the student the inner reserves needed to take the risk of trying with enthusiasm for the next learning. That next success pumps up the confidence bubble, which triggers more vigorous trying and more success. And so the cycle continues, with success feeding on success. The result is a student with a strong sense of academic self-efficacy. (p. 419)

How students view themselves has a profound effect on their self-worth, their motivation, and, ultimately, their learning. Kanter (2006) makes the case that "failure or success are not episodes, they are trajectories. They are tendencies, directions, pathways. Each decision . . . each school year seems like a new event, but the next performance is shaped by what happened last time out, unless something breaks that streak" (p. 9). How students perform on assessments, then, has the power to hold them on a preceding trajectory—be it success or failure—or to change course in how they see themselves as learners and, indeed, in their very learning potential. What that means to us as educators is that assessment and how we apply it in classrooms cannot be overlooked as a commanding influence on student achievement. Accept that truth, and the next step is to determine what constitutes effective assessment.

Attributes of Effective Assessment

Literacy outcomes are measured more than any other content area and "no other component of the curriculum has been subjected throughout its history to such intense controversy" (Venezky, 1987, p. 159). The debate circling around assessment has certainly not waned since Venezky's review of the modern history of reading instruction; if anything, assessment has pushed to the forefront as the most contentious issue in education today. Unfortunately, assessment has come to epitomize two disturbing trends: The only relevant assessment is high-stakes, standardized tests, and only these formal measures indicate the quality of teaching and learning.

Rather than be governed by large-scale assessments, consider the power of classroom assessments. Beyond the very real strength they possess to direct instructional actions; they also have the potential to increase average scores on standardized assessments by up to four grade equivalents or 15–20 percentile points (Stiggins, 1999). That is tremendous, and yet are we leveraging assessments to get at the root of student need, transform our instruction to be more prescriptive to those needs, and create an environment where they are accepted as an important part of the learning process for teachers as well as students? The answer, sadly, is no. We are not employing assessments to enhance the quality of our teaching or improve the learning of our students, but we can change that. Let's consider some of the key attributes of effective assessment planning.

Aligned to Instructional Purpose. Assessment is only valid when it is correlated to instruction. Otherwise, it is meaningless. Learning objectives and assessment are inseparable. While objectives state what students are expected to learn, it is the assessment tool that verifies if those expectations have been met.

It is also crucial to select the appropriate assessment to determine student learning. Choose an unsuitable assessment and skew your understanding of student learning. For example, if you want to ascertain students' reading comprehension skills, do not opt for an oral reading fluency instrument. Although fluency does have an incontrovertible link to reading comprehension, it will not provide an accurate representation of how well students make meaning from text. Likewise, a MAZE instrument (i.e., a timed, silently read cloze task), although engineered to measure comprehension, will not generate a true interpretation as it incorporates a multiple choice format that offers the potential for success based on probability and can be answered by analyzing sentence by sentence and not the passage as a whole (January & Ardoin, 2012).

Reflective of the Learning Process. Too often, we base our assessments on an end product. If assessment is to reflect real learning, it should highlight the thinking processes involved and offer ongoing feedback that delineates how to improve student performance. Thus, when planning for assessment, consider what opportunities you embed for students to demonstrate their personal learning process—their conceptions and misconceptions, the depth and breadth of their understanding, and their ability to apply new knowledge in novel and realistic contexts.

Flexible to Meet the Needs of Teachers, Students, and the Classroom. Assessment is not effective if it functions as a fixed entity without being responsive to the constantly shifting needs of the classroom. One assessment, no matter how comprehensive, simply cannot address the complex issues of teaching and learning. It is critical that assessment evolve alongside instruction. For instance, if a student scores well on an oral reading fluency assessment but is reading without any attention to phrase markers or punctuation or without any expression, you may be concerned that the fluency score is not truly indicative of the student's reading. In this scenario, it may helpful to hold a conference with the student to debrief about what was observed, ask for self-reflection to encourage the student to analyze what strategies were used, and identify what metacognitive skills the student possesses. To determine if comprehension is being affected by these identified fluency concerns, a brief oral retelling may provide additional understanding of the student's reading abilities. In effect, your assessment must be responsive to changing needs, clarifying what current skill sets exist and where to continue instruction. If assessment is to be useful to your instructional practice, it should be elastic . . . changing, adaptable, responsive.

Geared to Inform Instruction. Assessment for its own sake is useless. Unless it has some bearing on instruction, it has no value. If used correctly, however, it has the power to transform your teaching as you analyze the strengths and needs of your students and adjust your instruction accordingly.

To maximize its potential, assessment must adhere to three basic guidelines—assess more than one skill, be formative in nature, and represent multimodal assessments. A single-skill assessment lacks the strength to define student competencies. In order to glean an accurate understanding of the extent of student proficiency, assessments should analyze multiple skills in a variety of contexts and with a range of purposes. It must also take place during instruction—not after—if it is to leverage assessment into enhanced instruction and increased gains in performance. Neither can it influence student learning without acknowledging the literacy experiences that students have in school and at home. It is no longer a paper and pencil world; assessment should utilize not just the traditional paper and pencil format of the past but also embrace the electronic world of today.

Developed as Ongoing Cycle for Teaching and Learning. An effective instructional program must have an equally valuable assessment system. Just as our teaching strives to provide the best possible educational opportunities for our students, our assessments should ensure that we have the ability to provide targeted support and personalized learning experiences—that is only possible if you have a comprehensive literacy assessment profile of your students.

There are four components of a literacy assessment profile—screening, diagnosis, ongoing assessment, and outcome assessment—and none is useful without the other three. Each one has a distinctive purpose and is complementary to the others. One alone will never suffice to identify and address student abilities and needs. Together, however, it is possible to triangulate data to gather a complete evaluation of student learning. Screenings and diagnostics work in tandem to ensure students are identified for potential academic gaps while ongoing assessment continues to monitor student performance, and outcome assessment provides a concluding evaluation of student achievement and program effectiveness. Without this integration of multiple assessment pieces, "an assessment system can easily slip into a fragmented set of activities—assessment bits and pieces that are difficult to manage and use" (Roskos, 2004, p. 94). Table 10.1 illustrates the characteristics of each piece of the literacy assessment profile and how they function jointly to provide a complete understanding of student learning.

Screening. Screening typically originates at the beginning of the academic year, continues at pre-determined times throughout the year, and serves to identify starting points for instruction as well as to call attention to specific students who may struggle and would benefit from additional support. While all grades should use screening instruments to locate at-risk students, they have increasingly been called for in the primary grades as a tool for identification, prevention, and targeted instruction for students who may experience reading difficulties during the early stages of literacy development.

Common areas of interest for screenings encompass phonological and phonemic awareness, letter identification, phonics, spelling, vocabulary, oral reading fluency, and comprehension. Either formal or informal tools may be used, but screenings should always have pre-determined mastery targets.

TABLE 10.1 Literacy Assessment Profile Components

Assessment Component	Purpose	Timing	Frequency	Scope
Screening	Identify at-risk students	Prior to instruction	1–3 times yearly	Broad (All students)
Diagnosis	Pinpoint student needs	Prior to instruction; whenever deemed necessary	Subsequent to screening; whenever necessary	Specific (only identified students)
Ongoing Assessment	Inform and modify instruction to meet the needs of students	During instruction	Daily	Specific (all students, but concentrated on particular aspects of the curriculum)
Outcome Assessment	Evaluate student achievement and literacy program effectiveness	After instruction	Weekly; monthly; yearly	Broad (all students)

Diagnosis. As a follow-up to screenings in which students have been identified as at risk or at any other time when concerns are raised, diagnostic instruments determine what academic gaps exist and where instructional support can begin. These tools are utilized, then, to determine specific information about individual students and should provide enough insight to ensure that instruction can address their specific needs.

Ongoing assessment. Ongoing assessment encompasses prescribed progress monitoring for identified students receiving additional instructional support as well as formative assessments encompassing all students. This form of less formalized instruments is key because "just as standardized tests have produced a testing culture, educators interested in reform must recognize and examine the need for a classroom culture that will sustain the values, merits, and practices of more authentic forms of assessment" (McMahan & Gifford, 2001, p. 36).

Progress monitoring is a school-based, individualized assessment that gauges the degree to which students are making satisfactory progress and establishes if instruction needs to be tweaked. It typically takes place at regular intervals in response to prescriptive instruction and may include an ongoing appraisal of phonological or phonemic awareness, phonics, vocabulary, oral reading fluency, or comprehension—as well as a judgment on the students' potential to reach end-of-year, grade-level standards.

Formative assessment, on the other hand, comprises continuing checks of student understanding during instruction to guide the teaching process and modify experiences to increase student learning, and significantly, "it is only the consistent use of formative assessment . . . that has shown promise in improving student learning and achievement. . . . Even more importantly, formative assessment reduces the achievement gap by helping low achievers the most" (Volante & Beckett, 2011, p. 240). Researchers also credit formative assessment as a singularly powerful intervention to increase student achievement for second-language learners and students with special needs (Alvarez, Ananda, Walqui, Sato, & Rabinowitz, 2014; Laud, Hirsch, Patel, & Wagner, 2010).

What's more, formative assessment is carried out within the context of scaffolding so that you can consistently and intentionally move students to ever-increasing levels of academic growth based on their existing performance. Although effective instruction is pivotal, it is actually assessment that contributes to your ability to provide high-quality instruction at students' Zone of Proximal Development: If the assessment indicates a firm grasp of the material, then instruction can continue at a deeper level. However, a demonstration of partial mastery, suggests changes in instructional planning to accommodate student need. Roskos and Neuman (2012) actually contend that formative assessment is a "gap-minder" as it allows teachers to identify breaks between where students are currently and where they need to be and remain watchful of students and modify instruction as needed.

When do you use these gap-minders? Formative assessments are embedded within the instruction itself, but they can occur at three distinct points—before instruction, during instruction, and after instruction. Prior to beginning a lesson, students can complete a pretest to demonstrate what knowledge and competencies they already possess in order for you to adjust instructional planning. In the midst of teaching, you can use additional checks like questioning, thumbs up/thumbs down, or response cards to monitor understanding and guide instruction. At the end of instruction, students can complete exit slips expressing what they learned.

Outcome assessment. Outcome assessment also includes two elements—end-of-unit assessments and end-of-year assessments, such as with tests, final exams, cumulative projects, and high-stakes standardized tests. This form of assessment is distinguished by its purpose in evaluating both students and programs with no intent for immediate change in instruction. While it is essential to determine the effectiveness of the literacy program as well as the learning outcomes of students; it does not allow for a response to its results until after the teaching and learning process is complete. Thus, it offers the ability to make substantive changes—but those changes have no impact on learning within that moment of instructional time and consequently do not support the immediate needs of students.

Varied Means of Assessment

Although there are four major components of the literacy assessment profile, the number of assessment tools is much broader. Assessment does not, and should not, be restricted to the ubiquitous quizzes and tests found in nearly every classroom. The possibilities are abundant; it is up to you to utilize assessment tools to their greatest potential to maximize instruction. Remember that "the quickest way to change student learning is to change the assessment system" (Elton and Laurillard, 1979, p. 100). Below is a brief list of useful assessments that can be integrated into a literacy assessment portfolio.

Anecdotal Records. When creating a literacy assessment, anecdotal records offer a systematic method to note observations of students within a literacy environment. Creating such a document necessitates that the teacher record only observable behaviors with no inferences or judgments on the part of the observer

168 ◆ Ensuring Student Success

and writes in a way that clearly describes what the student was doing and saying during the observed time.

While conventional anecdotal records can provide a journalist-like objectivity and insight to student performance, selecting a particular focus will help you to maintain a critical lens through which to view students. More specifically, Boyd-Batstone (2004) contends that having a standards-based concentration allows the teacher to attend to what students can and cannot do in relation to particular content, and using the verbs embedded in content standards to document what students are doing facilitates data collection as well as highlights how expertly students are able to perform these standards. For example, a standard for Grade 1 expects a student to retell a narrative, demonstrating an understanding of the central message or theme. If the anecdotal record reflects that the student is struggling with relating the beginning, middle, and end, that directs the teacher to focus first on identifying major events before moving to key details. From that point, the teacher may then transition to the development of theme in stories.

It will also be helpful to evaluate how these observations may inform instructional practice in relation to these same standards. An observation marked with an *S* suggests an area of strength, one marked with an *N* designates an area of need, and one that has an *I* recorded indicates a point of information about the student (Boyd-Batstone, 2004). Implementing anecdotal records through this perspective heightens awareness of what it truly valued in the classroom as well as how to purpose them to inform instruction.

Constructed-Response Assessments. If you rely on standardized assessments, then you may not furnish students enough opportunities to demonstrate their learning to the fullest extent. Rather than choosing selected-response items (e.g., multiple choice, matching, true/false) where answers are provided and at least some aspect of a student's answer may well be based on probability and guessing, constructed-response items (e.g., short answer and brief essays) encourage students to think more deeply for themselves and learn how to relate their content knowledge in concise, evidence-based answers. These assessments are also much more greatly attuned to diagnosing student cognition as well as program effectiveness. As we have continued throughout this book to emphasize the process of student thinking and learning over the reliance of just an end product, constructed-response items allow us to understand the process that students undertake when engaged with content in place of the product of the simple selection of a multiple choice item.

In preparing constructed-response assessments, focus on the objective to be assessed and ensure that the item truly does measure what you want to discover about student learning. Also, remember that constructed-response assessments compel students to use more cognitive dexterity than a selected-response item, so the question should necessitate a student to express the depth of his or her understanding of a specific learning objective. Rubrics should also be developed to facilitate scoring in such a way that clearly delineates expectations and clarity.

Developmental Spelling Assessments. This instrument allows you to identify students' spelling skills, and more significantly, their awareness and expertise with phonics sounds and patterns, as well as morphological effects on words. It also provides insights into students' strengths and weaknesses in a way that cannot be communicated through a student's words alone.

Administered like a traditional spelling test, these inventories commonly contain word lists representing a variety of fundamental orthographic patterns (e.g., consonant blends and digraphs, short and long vowels, r-controlled vowels) and morphological patterns (e.g., prefixes and suffixes, including inflectional endings). After students have completed the assessment, your next step is to analyze the data to look for patterns and plan for instruction to target those areas in which a student may be struggling.

Early Literacy Assessments. As young children begin to acquire literacy skills, a screening comprising an array of discrete, skill-based assessments can offer crucial information to identify at-risk students and to prevent potential reading impediments. These instruments typically include measures for phonological and phonemic awareness, letter identification, phonics, and sight words. As foundational skills for subsequently more advanced reading competencies in fluency and comprehension, early literacy assessments should be a non-negotiable assessment in the primary classroom.

Essays. Essays are, in fact, extended constructed-response items. That said, they offer a greater likelihood that students can truly explore their own grasp of content materials at a deeper level of thinking, communicate that to the teacher, and offer a genuine sample for ascertaining student knowledge. Essays, however, are divided into separate and distinct types—reflective essays that ask students to demonstrate comprehension of content learned in classroom instruction and the timed, on-demand essays typically found in high-stakes assessments that require different instructional and assessment support.

Informal Reading Inventories. Commonly credited to the work of Emmett Betts in 1946, Informal Reading Inventories (IRIs) are one of the most prevalently used assessments in elementary and middle school classrooms, especially for the purpose of diagnosing a student's reading performance and identifying instructional levels. IRIs are a compilation of several assessments in one—word identification, oral reading fluency, and comprehension—which is individually administered to evaluate several facets of a student's reading performance. The word recognition is assessed through graded word lists. With the passages, assessment usually begins at the student's independent level and then progresses to more challenging text. The reading level of the student is then determined based on either the oral reading measure alone or sometimes in conjunction with reading comprehension questions or a retell linked to those same passages. A few IRIs also offer phonemic awareness and phonics assessment as well. Some schools elect to use IRIs as screening tools at the beginning of the academic year, as diagnosis instruments so that remediation can be offered for any identified at-risk students, and eventually as summative assessments to determine student growth over the course of the year. Well-respected IRIs include the Bader and Pearce (2013), Johns (2010), and the QRI (2001).

Objective Tests. Early educational experts who championed a "knowledge-based approach" to learning espoused the belief that learning was based on the rote memorization of basic skills.

The obvious way to assess their rote memory was to administer an objective test. Their beliefs evolved into the predominant way that we assess today. Easily administered and scored, these measurements have become the mainstay of standardized assessments, but there are real concerns about their use to drive instruction. Consisting of selected-response items (e.g., multiple choice, matching, listing), objective tests commonly elicit less cognitive rigor, but you can alter that paradigm by crafting selected-response items that compel students to reflect, infer, problem solve, and evaluate. You can also offer multiple correct options from which to select so that there is not just one correct possible answer, thus compelling students to think beyond one possible solution.

Also, be aware there is always the issue of the "anticipation effect" of objective tests versus constructed-response items. If students are notified in advance that an assessment will be objective, they tend to focus more on memorization or basic facts and details; in contrast, when alerted that they will be completing constructed response items (i.e., short answer and/or essay), students tend to concentrate on big ideas and a more global perspective of the content (Martinez, 1999). Writing more cognitively rigorous selected-response items, however, will reduce the impact of these dueling measures. Despite their inherent weaknesses, objective tests still function as one aspect of a literacy assessment portfolio.

Oral Reading Fluency Measures. Assessing oral reading fluency (ORF) centers on the role of fluency as a primary component of reading development. In this assessment, however, only automaticity (rate) and accuracy are tested; prosody (expressiveness) is not measured—nor is a student's ability to comprehend those words. ORF centers on word calling—not comprehension. In this measure, students are given an unfamiliar text and asked to read aloud for one minute. At the end of that minute, the administrator calculates the total numbers of words read correctly and subtracts the number of errors to determine the words correct per minute (WCPM).

Researchers suggest that fluency measures are particularly effective screening measures as they provide consistent appraisals of student reading performance efficiently and reliably. Although it is not typically used until the middle of the first grade, it offers a particularly strong correlation to comprehension for elementary and middle school students (Fuchs, Fuchs, Hosp, & Jenkins, 2001). While we would strongly discourage an ORF assessment to be used in isolation, it can offer another piece of information about student reading performance.

Oral Retelling. Oral retelling obliges students to comprehend and communicate the main elements of a text—that is, they must first determine the most important information to share, organize it in a coherent sequence, and articulate their response in a manner that demonstrates understanding. For younger students, oral reading offers a more authentic manner of assessing reading comprehension than posing isolated questions. It has been documented to be effective for all students, but especially for English language learners (Isbell, Sobol, Lindauer, & Lowrance, 2004; Sudweeks et al., 2004). Research has also revealed that oral retelling works just as effectively as an instructional strategy with students better able to answer both literal and inferential questions after retelling the text (Schisler, Joseph, Konrad, & Alber-Morgan, 2010).

Performance Assessments. To present a more accurate representation of students learning over more traditional methods, performance assessments engage students in authentic activities linked to real-world applications of content knowledge at the conclusion of which they produce a product or performance. Thus, rather than regurgitate rote memorization of concepts or individual prompts, students are presented with a series of tasks that oblige them to employ their learning. As with other measures, performance assessments should be linked to a specified learning objective with tasks designed for students to apply their learning across content areas and employ critical thinking and problem solving. This type of assessment can most easily be linked to the work students complete in project-based learning (PBL) projects.

Portfolios. In contrast to the snapshot effect of learning that most assessments produce, portfolios generate an entire scrapbook with varied artifacts (e.g., teacher observations, student work samples, photos, student reflections) from the classroom representing students' ongoing progress. This multifaceted collection of student work brings about a number of instructional benefits: 1) an authentic approach to assessment that depicts a realistic representation of learning; 2) self-reflection and self-assessment; 3) communication among students, teachers, and parents; and 4) empowerment for students in their own learning (Hall & Hewitt-Gervais, 2000). Portfolios can gain more instructional "muscle" when there is a clear learning purpose known to both the educator and the students, and all of the contributions reflect this central objective. Scoring and assessment criteria should also be determined prior to implementing portfolios so that the expectations are transparent and unambiguous.

Rubrics. Assessments utilizing rubrics are designed to be directly connected to instruction. With explicit statements denoting the criteria by which student work will be evaluated, rubrics offer clear expectations for students to guide their performance, descriptions of different levels of performance expertise, and opportunities for reflection and feedback. Researchers studying the writing performance of elementary students have also linked the use of rubrics to improved quality of writing (Cohen, Lotan, Scarloss, Shultz, & Abram, 2002).

Running Records. Intended to notate and analyze students' reading behaviors, running records present a student with an authentic text, in contrast to a prepared text intended for testing purposes, to read in an relaxed, untimed setting. As the student reads, the teacher works from a copy of the same text, noting the percentage of words read correctly and coding observed reading behaviors, such as repetitions, substitutions, omissions, self-corrections, etc.

Later, the teacher analyzes these coding marks to assess fluency, accuracy, and meaning as well to identify what cueing systems a student is using. Cues include meaning, syntax, and visual. Students who use meaning cues are aware that they can gain understanding of a text by looking at the accompanying visuals, considering whether a word makes sense in a given sentence, and determining if what they read makes sense in the passage's context. They are characterized by self-corrections when students realize that the words they have read do not make sense. Syntax cues encompass an understanding of grammar and the structure of English to assist in making meaning. Visual cues refer to the ability to recognize that the visual features of letters and words have a relationship to how they are spoken. Students' pronunciation should resemble the sounds (e.g., initial or ending) of the word. The expectation is that students who assimilate all three individual cueing systems into an integrated system can look at the visual aspect of a word to begin to sound it out while simultaneously checking for meaning and syntax. Running records become even more powerful when paired with a post-reading retelling or summary and a post-reading diagnostic conference.

Self-Assessments. As with the other facets of the Core Literacy Block, assessment should include a gradual release of responsibility. Self-assessment is a pivotal way to support that level of engagement as it "returns voice and ownership to students" (Bingham, Holbrook, & Meyers, 2010, p. 59) and is associated with increased involvement in their own learning and a greater grasp of content (Cauley & McMillan, 2010).

For self-assessments to be effective, students should not just evaluate their learning within the context of a content standard or instruction but also focus on their own metacognitive reflection, such as the thinking processes they employ, the skills they have in their repertoire, and the strategies they use to support their understanding. While some in the field express concerns about the class time need to complete these assessments, the reality is that self-assessments offer students a bridge from school expectations to their own personal learning and self-improvement (Bingham, Holbrook, & Meyers, 2010). It simply makes sense to encourage students to strive toward self-awareness and learn to analyze their work objectively (Roskos & Neuman, 2012).

Standardized Tests. Every assessment has a purpose and a place in the literacy assessment portfolio. Standardized tests are no different. They are pivotal in evaluating the instructional program, measuring identifiable standards, and locating trends in student learning. While we strongly support the belief that the bulk of assessments should be more authentic and student-centered in order to customize instruction in a way that supports individual growth, standardized tests do offer an objective evaluation of teaching and learning.

Conclusion

Researchers have suggested that educators devote from 30% to 50% of their time on assessment-related activities, such as with administration, analysis, intervention, and reporting; some even argue that it may reach up to an astounding 90% of their time (Campbell & Evans, 2000; Plake, 1993), and yet we are not taking advantage of the potential assessments we have as drivers for instruction. Creating a literacy assessment portfolio for each student that is aligned to and reflective of the learning process is the first step in making assessment important—for you and for your students. From a carefully selected collection of literacy measures, you can leverage those assessments to make the most of teaching and learning. Your students have untapped potential; you just need a re-envisioned literacy block to maximize your instruction and personalize their learning. Take the leap . . . and change the literacy lives of your students.

Appendices

- Appendix A: Literacy Block Schedules
- Appendix B: Phonics Development
- Appendix C: Morphology Study
- Appendix D: Common Core Standards

Appendix A

Literacy Block Schedules

45 minutes
(Typically Found in Grades 7–8)

15 minutes: Whole-Group Instruction
  5 minutes - Word Study
  5 minutes - Vocabulary
  5 minutes - Comprehension
30 minutes: Small-Group Instruction
  7–8 minutes - Guided Reading
  7–8 minutes - Word Study APP Center
  7–8 minutes - Vocabulary APP Center
  7–8 minutes - Comprehension APP Center

60 minutes
(Typically Found in Grade 6)

15 minutes: Whole-Group Instruction
  5 minutes - Word Study
  5 minutes - Vocabulary
  5 minutes - Comprehension
45 minutes: Small-Group Instruction
  10–11 minutes - Guided Reading
  10–11 minutes - Word Study APP Center
  10–11 minutes - Vocabulary APP Center
  10–11 minutes - Comprehension APP Center

Schedules

90 minutes
(Typically Found in Grades 3–5)

30 minutes: Whole-Group Instruction
  10 minutes - Word Study
  10 minutes - Vocabulary
  10 minutes - Comprehension
60 minutes: Small-Group Instruction
  15 minutes - Guided Reading
  15 minutes - Word Study APP Center
  15 minutes - Vocabulary APP Center
  15 minutes - Comprehension Center

120 minutes
(Typically Found in K–2)

30 minutes: Whole-Group Instruction
  10 minutes - Word Study
  10 minutes - Vocabulary
  10 minutes - Comprehension
90 minutes: Small - Group Instruction
  22–23 minutes - Guided Reading
  22–23 minutes - Word Study APP Center
  22–23 minutes - Vocabulary APP Center
  22–23 minutes - Comprehension APP Center

Appendix B
Phonics Development

Phonics	Examples		Grade-Level Benchmark
Letter Names (uppercase and lowercase)	a, b, c, d, e, f, g, h, i, j, k, l, m, n, o, p, q, r, s, t, u, v, w, x, y, z		Kindergarten
Letter Sounds (uppercase and lowercase)	a, b, c, d, e, f, g, h, i, j, k, l, m, n, o, p, q, r, s, t, u, v, w, x, y, z		Kindergarten
Short Vowels C-V-C	a = ă	cat	Grade 1
	e = ĕ	bed	
	i = ĭ	pig	
	o = ŏ	dog	
	u = ŭ	bug	
Consonant Blends (At Beginning of Words) C-C-V-C	L-Blends		Grade 1
	bl	blue	
	cl	clown	
	fl	fly	
	pl	plane	
	spl	splash	
	S-Blends		
	sc	scarf	
	sk	skip	
	sl	slam	

(Continued)

182 ◆ Appendix B

Phonics	Examples		Grade-Level Benchmark
	sp	spot	
	sm	small	
	sn	snail	
	sw	sweet	
	st	step	
	R-Blends		
	br	bring	
	cr	cry	
	dr	drag	
	fr	frog	
	gr	green	
	pr	pretty	
	tr	tree	
	scr	scratch	
	spr	spring	
	str	stream	
	Additional Blends		
	tw	twin	
	thr	throw	
	qu	queen	
	squ	squash	
Consonant Blends (at end of words) C-V-C-C	ct	act	Grade 1
	ft	draft	
	pt	apt	
	lb	bulb	
	ld	wild	
	lf	wolf	
	lk	bulk	
	lm	calm	
	lp	help	
	lt	tilt	
	mp	lamp	
	nd	kind	
	nt	tent	
	sk	ask	
	sp	gasp	
	st	cost	
Consonant Digraphs	ck	back	Grade 1
	ch	chop	
	sh	ship	
	th	thumb	
	tch	watch	
	wh	white	
Long Vowels (C-V-C-E)	$a = \bar{a}$	face	Grade 1
	$e = \bar{e}$	Pete	
	$i = \bar{i}$	bite	
	$o = \bar{o}$	note	
	$u = \bar{u}$	cube	

Appendix B ◆ 183

Phonics	Examples		Grade-Level Benchmark
Long Vowels (vowel digraphs)	ai = ā ay = ā ea = ē ee = ē ei = ē ey = ē ie = ī oa = ō ou = ō ow = ō	bait tray seat meet either key pie boat though blow	Grade 2
Vowel Diphthongs	au aw oi oo ou ow oy	author saw oil boot out cow boy	Grade 2
R-Controlled Vowels	ar er ir or ur	mark bigger dirt word burn	Grade 2
L-Controlled Vowels	al	talk	Grade 2
Soft C and G	c = /s/ sound (soft) c = /k/ sound (hard) g = /j/ sound (soft) g = /g/ sound (hard)	cent cap gym gum	Grade 2
Y Sounds	y = /y/ (at the beginning of a word) y = /ī/ (at the end of a one-syllable word) y = / ē/ (at the end of a multisyllabic word)	yellow sky funny	Grade 2
Silent Letters	bt = /t/ ck = / k/ gh = /g/ gn = /n/ kn = /n/ mb = /m/ sc = /s/ wr = /r/	doubt check ghost gnat knee climb scene write	Grade 2

(Continued)

184 ◆ Appendix B

Phonics	Examples		Grade-Level Benchmark
Schwa *Occurs in multisyllabic words in which the vowel sound changes similar to ŭ, or "uh."	a = ă e = ĕ i = ĭ o = ŏ u = ŭ	about elephant family above support	Grade 3
Syllable Types & Dividing Syllables *The number of vowel sounds equals the number of syllables in a word.	*Closed Syllable* Syllable ends in a consonant, and the vowel sound is short. C-V-C V-C-C-V	cat cab-in rab-bit	Grade 3
	Open Syllable Syllable ends in a vowel, and the vowel sound is long. C-V	me pho-to	
	Vowel-Consonant-E Syllable Syllable typically at the end of the word; the final e silent and the previous vowel is long. C-V-C-E	make mis-take	
	Vowel Team Syllable Syllable contains two vowels side by side that together make one sound. C-V-V-C	tray heat-er	
	Consonant + le Syllable Syllable containing a consonant plus the letters le.	a-ble tur-tle bub-ble	
	R-Controlled Syllable Syllable contains a vowel followed by an r. The r changes the way the vowel sounds.	farm bar-ter	

Appendix C
Morphology Study

Grade	Prefix	Root	Suffix	Definition	Example
1			-s	plural form of nouns, more than one	songs, cakes
			-es	plural form of nouns, more than one	catches, mashes
			-ies	plural form of nouns, more than one	puppies, parties, cries
			-ing	action occurring	catching, splashing
			-ed	past tense	jumped, liked
			-ied	past tense	tried
			-er	comparing of two items	richer, smarter
				person's profession	teacher, baker
			-est	comparing three or more items	richest, smartest

186 ◆ Appendix C

Grade	Prefix	Root	Suffix	Definition	Example
2	dis-			not, opposite of	dislike, disagree
	pre-			before	preschool, preplan
	re-			again	redo, return
	un-			not, remove of	uncertain, unfold
			-able	will be	likeable, agreeable
			-en	irregular nouns	oxen
			-en	to use the verb as a past participle	eaten
			-ful	full of	beautiful, helpful
			-less	not full of	helpless, tasteless
			-ness	state of being	sadness, helpfulness
			-s	to make verb agree with singular subject	child eats
			-'s	singular possessive	boy's book
			-s'	plural possessive	cats' paws

Grade	Prefix	Root	Suffix	Definition	Example
3	in-			not	inactive
	im-			not	impolite
	mis-			not good	mistake, misunderstand
	non-			not	nonstop, nonprofit
	over-			more than enough	overcook, overdo
	under-			not enough	undercook, underachieve
		-bio-		living things	biology, biosphere
		-cycl-		circle	cycle, cyclone
		-graph-		write	autograph, photograph
		-gram-		written down	diagram, grammar
		-photo-		light	photograph photosynthesis
		-phon-		sound	telephone, microphone
			-hood	state of being	neighborhood

Appendix C ◆ 187

Grade	Prefix	Root	Suffix	Definition	Example
			-ly	like	perfectly, honestly
			-ward	direction	backward
			-y	characterized by, like	bossy, fishy

Grade	Prefix	Root	Suffix	Definition	Example
4	bi-			two	bicycle, bilingual,
	co-			together, with	coauthor, coeducation
	col-			together, with	collect, collide
	com-			together, with	compare, community
	con-			together, with	conspire, contact
	de-			opposite	decrease, deconstruct
		-cert-		sure	certain, certify
		-fals-/ -fall-		wrong, lie	false, falsify
		-frac-		to break	fraction, fracture
		-equ-		fair, same	equalize
		-geo-		Earth	geology, geography
		-hemi-		half	hemisphere
		-loc-		place	locate, local
		-magn-		large	magnificent, magnify
		-meter-		measure	centimeter, speedometer
		-micro-		small	microscope
		-mim-		same	mimic, mime
		-min-		small	minimize, minute
			-al	relating to	geographical, illogical
			-en	to make	strengthen, weaken
			-ess	female	actress, lioness
			-hood	state of	childhood, neighborhood
			-ish	relating to	childish, selfish
			-ment	action result	movement, disappointment
			-or	person's profession	actor, doctor
			-tion	act of, state of being, result of	motivation, attention,

188 ◆ Appendix C

Grade	Prefix	Root	Suffix	Definition	Example
5	anti-			against	antisocial, antihero
	astro-			stars, space	astronaut, astronomy
	auto-			self, same	autobiography, automatic
	fore-			before	forecast, foreword
	milli-			one thousandth	millimeter, millisecond
	mono-			one, alone, single	monopoly, monosyllable
	multi-			more than one	multicultural, multimedia
	post-			after, later	postpone, postmark
	semi-			half	semicircle, semiannual
	sub-			below, under	subway, submarine
		-aud-		to hear	audio, audition
		-dict-		to say	diction, contradict
		-fin-		end	finish, finite
		-frater-		brother	fraternal, fraternity
		-ject-		throw	eject, reject
		-log-		word	dialogue, eulogy
		-mater-		mother	maternal, maternity
		-mit-		to send	transmit, emit
		-pater-		father	paternal, paternity
		-ped-		foot	pedometer, pedicure
		-struct-		build	construct, destruction
		-vid-		to see	video, evident
		-vis-		to see	visual, envision
			-an	profession, belonging to	electrician, American
			-able	capable of	breakable, laughable
			-ance	state of or quality of	brilliance, importance
			-ence	action or process	persistence, absence
			-ible	able, can	possible, responsible
			-ion	action, process	option, moderation
			-ive	given to	destructive, attractive
			-logy	study of	biology, zoology
			-ure	condition, process	measure, exposure

Appendix C ◆ 189

Grade	Prefix	Root	Suffix	Definition	Example
6	equ-			equal	equation, equidistant
	ex-			out, from	exit, exhume
	inter-			between, among	interstate, international
	macro-			large	macroevolution, macroeconomics
	mal-			bad, wrong	malicious, malcontent
	micro-			small	micrometer, microscopic
	per-			through, throughout	permanent, permeate
	pro-			for, in front of	promote, proceed
	pseudo-			false	pseudonym, pseudoscience
	retro-			back	retrospect, retroactive
	se-			apart, away from	secede, seclude
	super-			greater, over	superabundant, superstar
	trans-			across	transatlantic, transcontinental
	ultra-			extreme, beyond range	ultraviolet, ultramodern
	uni-			one	unify, unicorn
		-aqua-		water	aquatic, aquarium
		-bene-		good	benefactor, benefit
		-biblio-		book	bibliography, bibliophile
		-ceive-		to take hold	receive, deceive
		-ceed-		to go	proceed, exceed
		-cent-		hundred	century, centimeter
		-chron-		time	chronicle, chronology
		-cred-		believe	credit, credible
		-duct-		lead	abduct, conduct
		-dynam-		power	dynamic, dynamite
		-hydro-		water	dehydrate, hydroplane
		-mob-		move	mobile, immobilize
		-mot-		move	automotive, motion

(Continued)

190 ◆ Appendix C

Grade	Prefix	Root	Suffix	Definition	Example
		-mort-		death	mortal, mortician
		-nym-		name, word	acronym, synonym
		-phon-		sound	telephone, symphony
		-port-		to carry	transport, report
		-scope-		instrument for viewing	telescope, microscope
		-scrib-		write	scribble, transcribe
		-therm-		heat	thermostat, thermos
		-tract-		draw	distract, attract
		-vac-		empty	vacant, vacation
			-age	action, process	drainage, pilgrimage
			-aholic	one with obsession	workaholic, shopaholic
			-an	belong to	Italian, urban
			-ant/-ent	one who (often noun)	immigrant, resident
			-ent	perform, causes	absorbent, correspondent
			-ify	to become	intensify
			-ize	to make, to cause to become	authorize, apologize, energize
			-ous	full of	adventurous, mysterious
			-some	characterized by	worrisome, troublesome
			-ty	state of	honesty, stability

Grade	Prefix	Root	Suffix	Definition	Example
7	act-			do	activity, react
	agri-			land	agriculture, agrarian
	ambi-			both	ambidextrous, ambiguous
	bene-			good	benefactor, benevolent
	cent-			one hundred	century, centurion
	circ-			around	circumference, circumnavigate

Grade	Prefix	Root	Suffix	Definition	Example
	counter-			against	counteract
	deca-/ deci-			ten	decade, deciliter
	dys-			difficult, ill	dysfunctional, dysentery
	hecto-			one hundred	hectogram
	hexa-			six	hexagon, hexapod
	hyper-			over	hypersensitive, hyperactive
	il-			not	illegible, illegal
	octa-			eight	octagon, octave
	pent-			five	pentagon, pentathlon
	poly-			more than one, many	polygon, polyglot
	psych-			spirit, mind	psychic, psychologist
	quad-/ tetra-			four	quadrilateral, tetragon
	sept-			seven	septennial
		-chrome-		color	monochrome, chromosome
		-cogn-		to know	recognize, cognition
		-cur-		run	current, incur
		-dem-		people	democracy, epidemic
		-domin-		master	dominant, domineer
		-fac-		make	factory, benefactor
		-form-		shape	formulate, conform
		-gon-		side	polygon
		-grad-		step, stage	gradual, gradient
		-grav-		weighty	gravity, aggravate
		-lateral-		side	quadrilateral
		-mega-/ -magna-		large, powerful	megaphone, magnify
		-mem-		remember	memento, memoir
		-mut-		to change	mutation
		-pan-		all	pandemic
		-phob-		fear	phobia, arachnophobia

(Continued)

Grade	Prefix	Root	Suffix	Definition	Example
		-plan-		flat	plane, plantation
		-poli-/ -polis-		city, government	police, politician, metropolis
		-pot-		power	potential, potent
		-sphere-		ball	sphere, hemisphere
			-ic	characterized by, related to	realistic, historic
			-ism	belief in	pacifism, socialism
			-ist	person believes in	socialist, pacifist
			-logy	study of, field of	biology, psychology
			-trophy	nourishment, development	atrophy, dystrophy
			-tude	state or quality	aptitude, fortitude

Grade	Prefix	Root	Suffix	Definition	Example
8	ab-			not	abnormal
	agri-			field	agrarian, agribusiness
	ante-			before	anterior, antebellum
	anthro-			man	philanthropy, anthropology
	auto-			self	autocrat
	contra-			against	contradict
	dia-			through, across	diameter, diagnosis
	hetero-			different	heterogeneous, heterozygote
	homo-			same	homogeneous, homogenized
	kilo-			thousand	kilogram, kilowatt
	numer-			number	numerous, numerology

Grade	Prefix	Root	Suffix	Definition	Example
	omni-/ pan-			all	omnivore, pantheon
	paleo-			prehistoric	paleontology, paleography
	para-			beside	compare, parallel
	peri-			around	perimeter
	proto-			first	protozoan
		-auto-		self, oneself	autocracy, autodidact
		-belli-		war	rebellion, bellicose
		-cardo-		heart	cardiac,
		-chron-		time	chronic, chronological
		-con-		with, together	concerted, concur
		-derma-		skin	epidermis
		-ego-		I	egoism, egocentrism
		-ethno-		people	ethnicity, ethnology
		-fac-		to made, or do	manufacture, benefactor
		-helio-		sun	heliotrope
		-herb-		plant	herbivore
		-inter-		between, among	interstate, international
		-intra-		inside, within	intrastate, intravenous
		-lab-		work	collaborate, elaborate
		-nav-		ship	navy, navigate
		-neo-		new, revived	Neolithic, neonatal
		-omni-		all	omniscient
		-pend-		to hang	impending, appendage
		-pod-		foot	podiatrist, pseudo pod
		-port-		to carry	porter, import
		-sol-/-soli-		alone	solitary, solitude

(*Continued*)

Grade	Prefix	Root	Suffix	Definition	Example
		-syn-		to join	synapse, photosynthesis
		-test-		witness, affirm	testify, testimony
		-troph-		to eat	autotrophic
		-therm-		heat	thermometer, thermonuclear
		-tract-		to pull	attract, extract, subtract
		-vac-		empty	vacuum, vacant, evacuate
		-vid-/-vis-		to see	televise, supervise, evident
			-cide	kill	herbicide
			-ee	object of action	payee, employee
			-et/-ette	small	dinette, diskette
			-ide	chemical	sulfide, chloride

Appendix D

Common Core Standards

Key Ideas & Details	Standard 1	Standard 2	Standard 3
	Read closely to determine what the text says explicitly and to make logical inferences from it; cite specific textual evidence when writing or speaking to support conclusions drawn from the text.	*Determine central ideas or themes of a text and analyze their development; summarize the key supporting details and ideas.*	*Analyze how and why individuals, events, or ideas develop and interact over the course of a text.*
Kindergarten	With prompting and support, ask and answer questions about key details in a text.	With prompting and support, retell familiar stories, including key details; with prompting and support, identify the main topic and retell key details of a text.	With prompting and support, identify characters, settings, and major events in a story; with prompting and support, describe the connection between two individuals, events, ideas, or pieces of information in a text.

(Continued)

196 ◆ Appendix D

Key Ideas & Details	Standard 1	Standard 2	Standard 3
	Read closely to determine what the text says explicitly and to make logical inferences from it; cite specific textual evidence when writing or speaking to support conclusions drawn from the text.	*Determine central ideas or themes of a text and analyze their development; summarize the key supporting details and ideas.*	*Analyze how and why individuals, events, or ideas develop and interact over the course of a text.*
Grade 1	Ask and answer questions about key details in a text.	Retell stories, including key details, and demonstrate understanding of their central message or lesson; identify the main topic and retell key details of a text.	Describe characters, settings, and major events in a story, using key details; describe the connection between two individuals, events, ideas, or pieces of information in a text.
Grade 2	Ask and answer such questions as *who, what, where, when, why,* and *how* to demonstrate understanding of key details in a text.	Recount stories, including fables and folktales from diverse cultures, and determine their central message, lesson, or moral; identify the main topic of a multi-paragraph text as well as the focus of specific paragraphs within the text.	Describe how characters in a story respond to major events and challenges; describe the connection between a series of historical events, scientific ideas or concepts, or steps in technical procedures in a text.
Grade 3	Ask and answer questions to demonstrate understanding of a text, referring explicitly to the text as the basis for the answers.	Recount stories, including fables, folktales, and myths from diverse cultures; determine the central message, lesson, or moral and explain how it is conveyed through key	Describe characters in a story (e.g., their traits, motivations, or feelings) and explain how their actions contribute to the sequence of events; describe

Key Ideas & Details	Standard 1	Standard 2	Standard 3
	Read closely to determine what the text says explicitly and to make logical inferences from it; cite specific textual evidence when writing or speaking to support conclusions drawn from the text.	*Determine central ideas or themes of a text and analyze their development; summarize the key supporting details and ideas.*	*Analyze how and why individuals, events, or ideas develop and interact over the course of a text.*
		details in the text; determine the main idea of a text; recount the key details and explain how they support the main idea.	the relationship between a series of historical events, scientific ideas or concepts, or steps in technical procedures in a text, using language that pertains to time, sequence, and cause/effect.
Grade 4	Refer to details and examples in a text when explaining what the text says explicitly and when drawing inferences from the text.	Determine a theme of a story, drama, or poem from details in the text; determine the main idea of a text and explain how it is supported by key details; summarize the text.	Describe in depth a character, setting, or event in a story or drama, drawing on specific details in the text (e.g., a character's thoughts, words, or actions); explain events, procedures, ideas, or concepts in a historical, scientific, or technical text, including what happened and why, based on specific information in the text.

(Continued)

198 ◆ Appendix D

Key Ideas & Details	Standard 1	Standard 2	Standard 3
	Read closely to determine what the text says explicitly and to make logical inferences from it; cite specific textual evidence when writing or speaking to support conclusions drawn from the text.	*Determine central ideas or themes of a text and analyze their development; summarize the key supporting details and ideas.*	*Analyze how and why individuals, events, or ideas develop and interact over the course of a text.*
Grade 5	Quote accurately from a text when explaining what the text says explicitly and when drawing inferences from the text.	Determine a theme of a story, drama, or poem from details in the text, including how characters in a story or drama respond to challenges or how the speaker in a poem reflects upon a topic; determine two or more main ideas of a text and explain how they are supported by key details; summarize the text.	Compare and contrast two or more characters, settings, or events in a story or drama, drawing on specific details in the text (e.g., how characters interact); explain the relationships or interactions between two or more individuals, events, ideas, or concepts in a historical, scientific, or technical text based on specific information in the text.
Grade 6	Cite textual evidence to support analysis of what the text says explicitly as well as inferences drawn from the text.	Determine a theme or central idea of a text and how it is conveyed through particular details; determine a central idea of a text and how it is conveyed through particular details; provide a summary of the	Describe how a particular story's or drama's plot unfolds in a series of episodes as well as how the characters respond or change as the plot moves toward a resolution; analyze in detail how a key

Key Ideas & Details	Standard 1	Standard 2	Standard 3
	Read closely to determine what the text says explicitly and to make logical inferences from it; cite specific textual evidence when writing or speaking to support conclusions drawn from the text.	*Determine central ideas or themes of a text and analyze their development; summarize the key supporting details and ideas.*	*Analyze how and why individuals, events, or ideas develop and interact over the course of a text.*
		text distinct from personal opinions or judgments.	individual, event, or idea is introduced, illustrated, and elaborated in a text (e.g., through examples or anecdotes).
Grade 7	Cite several pieces of textual evidence to support analysis of what the text says explicitly as well as inferences drawn from the text.	Determine a theme or central idea of a text and analyze its development over the course of the text; determine two or more central ideas in a text and analyze their development over the course of the text; provide an objective summary of the text.	Analyze how particular elements of a story or drama interact (e.g., how setting shapes the characters or plot); analyze the interactions between individuals, events, and ideas in a text (e.g., how ideas influence individuals or events, or how individuals influence ideas or events).
Grade 8	Cite the textual evidence that most strongly supports an analysis of what the text says explicitly as well as inferences drawn from the text.	Determine a theme or central idea of a text and analyze its development over the course of the text, including its	Analyze how particular lines of dialogue or incidents in a story or drama propel the action, reveal aspects

(Continued)

200 ◆ Appendix D

Key Ideas & Details	Standard 1	Standard 2	Standard 3
	Read closely to determine what the text says explicitly and to make logical inferences from it; cite specific textual evidence when writing or speaking to support conclusions drawn from the text.	Determine central ideas or themes of a text and analyze their development; summarize the key supporting details and ideas.	Analyze how and why individuals, events, or ideas develop and interact over the course of a text.
		relationship to the characters, setting, and plot; determine a central idea of a text and analyze its development over the course of the text, including its relationship to supporting ideas; provide an objective summary of the text.	of a character, or provoke a decision; analyze how a text makes connections among and distinctions between individuals, ideas, or events (e.g., through comparisons, analogies, or categories).

Craft & Structure	Standard 4	Standard 5	Standard 6
	Interpret words and phrases as they are used in a text, including determining technical, connotative, and figurative meanings, and analyze how specific word choices shape meaning or tone.	Analyze the structure of texts, including how specific sentences, paragraphs, and larger portions of the text (e.g., a section, chapter, scene, or stanza) relate to each other and the whole.	Assess how point of view or purpose shapes the content and style of a text.
Kindergarten	Ask and answer questions about unknown words in a text; with prompting and support, ask and answer questions about unknown words in a text.	Recognize common types of texts (e.g., storybooks, poems); identify the front cover, back cover, and title page of a book.	With prompting and support, name the author and illustrator of a story and define the role of each in telling the story; name

Appendix D ◆ 201

Craft & Structure	Standard 4	Standard 5	Standard 6
	Interpret words and phrases as they are used in a text, including determining technical, connotative, and figurative meanings, and analyze how specific word choices shape meaning or tone.	*Analyze the structure of texts, including how specific sentences, paragraphs, and larger portions of the text (e.g., a section, chapter, scene, or stanza) relate to each other and the whole.*	*Assess how point of view or purpose shapes the content and style of a text.*
			the author and illustrator of a text and define the role of each in presenting the ideas or information in a text.
Grade 1	Identify words and phrases in stories or poems that suggest feelings or appeal to the senses; ask and answer questions to help determine or clarify the meaning of words and phrases in a text.	Explain major differences between books that tell stories and books that give information, drawing on a wide reading of a range of text types; know and use various text features (e.g., headings, tables of contents, glossaries, electronic menus, icons) to locate key facts or information in a text.	Identify who is telling the story at various points in a text; distinguish between information provided by pictures or other illustrations and information provided by the words in a text.

(*Continued*)

202 ◆ Appendix D

Craft & Structure	Standard 4	Standard 5	Standard 6
	Interpret words and phrases as they are used in a text, including determining technical, connotative, and figurative meanings, and analyze how specific word choices shape meaning or tone.	*Analyze the structure of texts, including how specific sentences, paragraphs, and larger portions of the text (e.g., a section, chapter, scene, or stanza) relate to each other and the whole.*	*Assess how point of view or purpose shapes the content and style of a text.*
Grade 2	Describe how words and phrases (e.g., regular beats, alliteration, rhymes, repeated lines) supply rhythm and meaning in a story, poem, or song; determine the meaning of words and phrases in a text.	Describe the overall structure of a story, including describing how the beginning introduces the story and the ending concludes the action; know and use various text features (e.g., captions, bold print, subheadings, glossaries, indexes, electronic menus, icons) to locate key facts or information in a text efficiently.	Acknowledge differences in the points of view of characters, including by speaking in a different voice for each character when reading dialogue aloud; identify the main purpose of a text, including what the author wants to answer, explain, or describe.
Grade 3	Determine the meaning of words and phrases as they are used in a text, distinguishing literal from non-literal language; determine the meaning of general academic and domain-specific words and phrases in a text.	Refer to parts of stories, dramas, and poems when writing or speaking about a text, using terms such as chapter, scene, and stanza; describe how each successive part builds on earlier sections; use text features and search	Distinguish their own point of view from that of the narrator or those of the characters; distinguish their own point of view from that of the author of a text.

Appendix D ◆ 203

Craft & Structure	Standard 4	Standard 5	Standard 6
	Interpret words and phrases as they are used in a text, including determining technical, connotative, and figurative meanings, and analyze how specific word choices shape meaning or tone.	*Analyze the structure of texts, including how specific sentences, paragraphs, and larger portions of the text (e.g., a section, chapter, scene, or stanza) relate to each other and the whole.*	*Assess how point of view or purpose shapes the content and style of a text.*
		tools (e.g., key words, sidebars, hyperlinks) to locate information relevant to a given topic efficiently.	
Grade 4	Determine the meaning of words and phrases as they are used in a text, including those that allude to significant characters found in mythology (e.g., Herculean); determine the meaning of general academic and domain-specific words or phrases in a text.	Explain major differences between poems, drama, and prose, and refer to the structural elements of poems (e.g., verse, rhythm, meter) and drama (e.g., casts of characters, settings, descriptions, dialogue, stage directions) when writing or speaking about a text; describe the overall structure (e.g., chronology, comparison, cause/effect, problem/solution) of events, ideas, concepts, or information in a text or part of a text.	Compare and contrast the point of view from which different stories are narrated, including the difference between first- and third-person narrations; compare and contrast a firsthand and secondhand account of the same event or topic; describe the differences in focus and the information provided.

(Continued)

204 ◆ Appendix D

Craft & Structure	Standard 4	Standard 5	Standard 6
	Interpret words and phrases as they are used in a text, including determining technical, connotative, and figurative meanings, and analyze how specific word choices shape meaning or tone.	*Analyze the structure of texts, including how specific sentences, paragraphs, and larger portions of the text (e.g., a section, chapter, scene, or stanza) relate to each other and the whole.*	*Assess how point of view or purpose shapes the content and style of a text.*
Grade 5	Determine the meaning of words and phrases as they are used in a text, including figurative language such as metaphors and similes; determine the meaning of general academic and domain-specific words and phrases in a text.	Explain how a series of chapters, scenes, or stanzas fits together to provide the overall structure of a particular story, drama, or poem; compare and contrast the overall structure (e.g., chronology, comparison, cause/effect, problem/solution) of events, ideas, concepts, or information in two or more texts.	Describe how a narrator's or speaker's point of view influences how events are described; analyze multiple accounts of the same event or topic, noting important similarities and differences in the point of view they represent.
Grade 6	Determine the meaning of words and phrases as they are used in a text, including figurative and connotative meanings; analyze the impact of a specific word choice on meaning and tone; determine the meaning of words and phrases as they are used in a text, including figurative, connotative, and technical meanings.	Analyze how a particular sentence, chapter, scene, or stanza fits into the overall structure of a text and contributes to the development of the theme, setting, or plot; analyze how a particular sentence, paragraph, chapter, or section	Explain how an author develops the point of view of the narrator or speaker in a text; determine an author's point of view or purpose in a text and explain how it is conveyed in the text.

Appendix D ◆ 205

Craft & Structure	Standard 4	Standard 5	Standard 6
	Interpret words and phrases as they are used in a text, including determining technical, connotative, and figurative meanings, and analyze how specific word choices shape meaning or tone.	*Analyze the structure of texts, including how specific sentences, paragraphs, and larger portions of the text (e.g., a section, chapter, scene, or stanza) relate to each other and the whole.*	*Assess how point of view or purpose shapes the content and style of a text.*
		fits into the overall structure of a text and contributes to the development of the ideas.	
Grade 7	Determine the meaning of words and phrases as they are used in a text, including figurative and connotative meanings; analyze the impact of rhymes and other repetitions of sounds (e.g., alliteration) on a specific verse or stanza of a poem or section of a story or drama; determine the meaning of words and phrases as they are used in a text, including figurative, connotative, and technical meanings; analyze the impact of a specific word choice on meaning and tone.	Analyze how a drama's or poem's form or structure (e.g., soliloquy, sonnet) contributes to its meaning; analyze the structure an author uses to organize a text, including how the major sections contribute to the whole and to the development of the ideas.	Analyze how an author develops and contrasts the points of view of different characters or narrators in a text; determine an author's point of view or purpose in a text and analyze how the author distinguishes his or her position from that of others.
Grade 8	Determine the meaning of words and phrases as they are used in a text, including figurative and connotative meanings; analyze the impact of specific word choices	Compare and contrast the structure of two or more texts and analyze how the differing structure of each	Analyze how differences in the points of view of the characters and the audience or reader (e.g., created

(Continued)

206 ◆ Appendix D

Craft & Structure	Standard 4	Standard 5	Standard 6
	Interpret words and phrases as they are used in a text, including determining technical, connotative, and figurative meanings, and analyze how specific word choices shape meaning or tone.	*Analyze the structure of texts, including how specific sentences, paragraphs, and larger portions of the text (e.g., a section, chapter, scene, or stanza) relate to each other and the whole.*	*Assess how point of view or purpose shapes the content and style of a text.*
	on meaning and tone, including analogies or allusions to other texts; determine the meaning of words and phrases as they are used in a text, including figurative, connotative, and technical meanings; analyze the impact of specific word choices on meaning and tone, including analogies or allusions to other texts.	text contributes to its meaning and style; analyze in detail the structure of a specific paragraph in a text, including the role of particular sentences in developing and refining a key concept.	through the use of dramatic irony) create such effects as suspense or humor; an author's point of view or purpose in a text and analyze how the author acknowledges and responds to conflicting evidence or viewpoints.

Appendix D ◆ 207

Integration of Knowledge & Ideas	Standard 7	Standard 8	Standard 9
	Integrate and evaluate content presented in diverse media and formats, including visually and quantitatively, as well as in words.	*Delineate and evaluate the argument and specific claims in a text, including the validity of the reasoning as well as the relevance and sufficiency of the evidence.*	*Analyze how two or more texts address similar themes or topics in order to build knowledge or to compare the approaches the authors take.*
Kindergarten	With prompting and support, describe the relationship between illustrations and the story in which they appear (e.g., what moment in a story an illustration depicts; with prompting and support, describe the relationship between illustrations and the text in which they appear (e.g., what person, place, thing, or idea in the text an illustration depicts).	With prompting and support, identify the reasons an author gives to support points in a text.	With prompting and support, compare and contrast the adventures and experiences of characters in familiar stories; with prompting and support, identify basic similarities in and differences between two texts on the same topic (e.g., in illustrations, descriptions, or procedures).
Grade 1	Use illustrations and details in a story to describe its characters, setting, or events; use the illustrations and details in a text to describe its key ideas.	Identify the reasons an author gives to support points in a text.	Compare and contrast the adventures and experiences of characters in stories; identify basic similarities in and differences

(Continued)

208 ◆ Appendix D

Integration of Knowledge & Ideas	Standard 7	Standard 8	Standard 9
	Integrate and evaluate content presented in diverse media and formats, including visually and quantitatively, as well as in words.	*Delineate and evaluate the argument and specific claims in a text, including the validity of the reasoning as well as the relevance and sufficiency of the evidence.*	*Analyze how two or more texts address similar themes or topics in order to build knowledge or to compare the approaches the authors take.*
			between two texts on the same topic (e.g., in illustrations, descriptions, or procedures).
Grade 2	Use information gained from the illustrations and words in a print or digital text to demonstrate understanding of its characters, setting, or plot; explain how specific images (e.g., a diagram showing how a machine works) contribute to and clarify a text.	Describe how reasons support specific points the author makes in a text.	Compare and contrast two or more versions of the same story (e.g., Cinderella stories) by different authors or from different cultures; compare and contrast the most important points presented by two texts on the same topic.
Grade 3	Explain how specific aspects of a text's illustrations contribute to what is conveyed by the words in a story (e.g., create mood, emphasize aspects of a character or setting); use	Describe the logical connection between particular sentences and paragraphs in a text (e.g., comparison, cause/effect, first/second/third in a sequence).	Compare and contrast the themes, settings, and plots of stories written by the same author about the same or similar characters (e.g., in books from a series); compare and contrast the most important

Integration of Knowledge & Ideas	Standard 7	Standard 8	Standard 9
	Integrate and evaluate content presented in diverse media and formats, including visually and quantitatively, as well as in words.	*Delineate and evaluate the argument and specific claims in a text, including the validity of the reasoning as well as the relevance and sufficiency of the evidence.*	*Analyze how two or more texts address similar themes or topics in order to build knowledge or to compare the approaches the authors take.*
	information gained from illustrations (e.g., maps, photographs) and the words in a text to demonstrate understanding of the text (e.g., where, when, why, and how key events occur).		points and key details presented in two texts on the same topic.
Grade 4	Make connections between the text of a story or drama and a visual or oral presentation of the text, identifying where each version reflects specific descriptions and directions in the text; compare and contrast a firsthand and secondhand account of the same event or topic; describe the differences in focus and the information provided.	Explain how an author uses reasons and evidence to support particular points in a text.	Compare and contrast the treatment of similar themes and topics (e.g., opposition of good and evil) and patterns of events (e.g., the quest) in stories, myths, and traditional literature from different cultures; integrate information from two texts on the same topic in order to write or speak about the subject knowledgeably.

(Continued)

210 ◆ Appendix D

Integration of Knowledge & Ideas	Standard 7	Standard 8	Standard 9
	Integrate and evaluate content presented in diverse media and formats, including visually and quantitatively, as well as in words.	Delineate and evaluate the argument and specific claims in a text, including the validity of the reasoning as well as the relevance and sufficiency of the evidence.	Analyze how two or more texts address similar themes or topics in order to build knowledge or to compare the approaches the authors take.
Grade 5	Analyze how visual and multimedia elements contribute to the meaning, tone, or beauty of a text (e.g., graphic novel, multimedia presentation of fiction, folktale, myth, poem); draw on information from multiple print or digital sources, demonstrating the ability to locate an answer to a question quickly or to solve a problem efficiently.	Explain how an author uses reasons and evidence to support particular points in a text, identifying which reasons and evidence support which point(s).	Compare and contrast stories in the same genre (e.g., mysteries and adventure stories) on their approaches to similar themes and topics; integrate information from several texts on the same topic in order to write or speak about the subject knowledgeably.
Grade 6	Compare and contrast the experience of reading a story, drama, or poem to listening to or viewing an audio, video, or live version of the text, including contrasting what they "see"	Trace and evaluate the argument and specific claims in a text, distinguishing claims that are supported by reasons and evidence from claims that are not.	Compare and contrast texts in different forms or genres (e.g., stories and poems; historical novels and fantasy stories) in terms of their approaches to similar themes and topics;

Appendix D ◆ 211

Integration of Knowledge & Ideas	Standard 7	Standard 8	Standard 9
	Integrate and evaluate content presented in diverse media and formats, including visually and quantitatively, as well as in words.	Delineate and evaluate the argument and specific claims in a text, including the validity of the reasoning as well as the relevance and sufficiency of the evidence.	Analyze how two or more texts address similar themes or topics in order to build knowledge or to compare the approaches the authors take.
	and "hear" when reading the text to what they perceive when they listen or watch; integrate information presented in different media or formats (e.g., visually, quantitatively) as well as in words to develop a coherent understanding of a topic or issue.		compare and contrast one author's presentation of events with that of another (e.g., a memoir written by and a biography on the same person).
Grade 7	Compare and contrast a written story, drama, or poem to its audio, filmed, staged, or multimedia version, analyzing the effects of techniques unique to each medium (e.g., lighting, sound, color, or camera focus and angles in a film); compare and contrast a text to	Trace and evaluate the argument and specific claims in a text, assessing whether the reasoning is sound and the evidence is relevant and sufficient to support the claims.	Compare and contrast a fictional portrayal of a time, place, or character and a historical account of the same period as a means of understanding how authors of fiction use or alter history; analyze how two or more authors writing about the same topic shape their

(Continued)

212 ◆ Appendix D

Integration of Knowledge & Ideas	Standard 7	Standard 8	Standard 9
	Integrate and evaluate content presented in diverse media and formats, including visually and quantitatively, as well as in words.	*Delineate and evaluate the argument and specific claims in a text, including the validity of the reasoning as well as the relevance and sufficiency of the evidence.*	*Analyze how two or more texts address similar themes or topics in order to build knowledge or to compare the approaches the authors take.*
	an audio, video, or multimedia version of the text, analyzing each medium's portrayal of the subject (e.g., how the delivery of a speech affects the impact of the words.		presentations of key information by emphasizing different evidence or advancing different interpretations of facts.
Grade 8	Analyze the extent to which a filmed or live production of a story or drama stays faithful to or departs from the text or script, evaluating the choices made by the director or actors; evaluate the advantages and disadvantages of using different mediums (e.g., print or digital text, video, multimedia) to present a particular topic or idea.	Delineate and evaluate the argument and specific claims in a text, assessing whether the reasoning is sound and the evidence is relevant and sufficient; recognize when irrelevant evidence is introduced.	Analyze how a modern work of fiction draws on themes, patterns of events, or character types from myths, traditional stories, or religious works such as the Bible, including describing how the material is rendered new; analyze a case in which two or more texts provide conflicting information on the same topic and identify where the texts disagree on matters of fact or interpretation.

References

Adams, M. (1990). *Beginning to read*. Cambridge, MA: MIT Press.

Adams, M. J., Foorman, B. R., Lundberg, I., & Beeler, T. (1998). *Phonemic awareness in young children*. Baltimore, MD: Brookes.

Alacapinar, F. (2008). Effectiveness of project-based learning. *Eurasian Journal of Educational Research, 32*, 17–35.

Albright, L. K., & Ariail, M. (2005). Tapping the potential of teacher read alouds in middle school. *Journal of Adolescent & Adult Literacy, 48*(7), 582–591.

Allington, R. L. (2001). *What really matters for struggling readers*. New York, NY: Longman.

Allington, R. L. (2009). If they don't read much . . . 30 years later. In E. H. Hiebert (Ed.), *Reading more, reading better* (pp. 30–54). New York, NY: Guilford.

Allington, R. L. (2013). What really matters when working with struggling readers. *The Reading Teacher, 66*(7), 520–530. doi: 10.1002/TRTR.1154

Allington, R. L., & Gabriel, R. E. (2012). Every child. Every day. *Educational Leadership, 69*(6), 10–15.

Almasi, J. F., Arya, P., & O'Flahavan, J. F. (2001). A comparative analysis of student and teacher development in more and less proficient discussions of literature. *Reading Research Quarterly, 36*(2), 96–120. doi: 10.1598/RRQ.36.2.1

Alvarez, L., Ananda, S., Walqui, A., Sato, E., & Rabinowitz, S. (2014). *Focusing formative assessment on the needs of English language learners*. San Francisco, CA: WestEd.

Amiryousefi, M., & Ketabi, S. (2011). Mnemonic instruction: A way to boost vocabulary learning and recall. *Journal of Language Teaching and Research, 2*(1), 178–182. doi: 10.4304/jltr.2.1.178–182

Anderson, L. M., Brubaker, N. L., Alleman-Brooks, J., & Duffy, G. G. (1985). A qualitative study of seatwork in first-grade classrooms. *The Elementary School Journal, 86*(2), 123–140.

Anderson, R., Hiebert, E. H., Scott, J. A., & Wilkinson, I. A. G. (1985). *Becoming a nation of readers: The report of the Commission on Reading*. Washington, DC: National Institute of Education, U.S. Department of Education.

Ankrum, J. W., & Bean, R. M. (2008). Differentiated reading instruction: What and how. *Reading Horizons, 48*(2), 133–146.

Applebee, A. N., & Langer, J. A. (2011). A snapshot of writing instruction in middle schools and high schools. *English Journal, 100*(6), 14–27.

Avalos, M. A., Plasencia, A., Chavez, C., & Rascón, J. (2007). Modified guided reading: Gateway to English as a second language and literacy learning. *The Reading Teacher, 61*(4), 318–329. doi: 10/1598/RT.61.4.4

Bader, L. A., & Pearce, D. L. (2013). *Bader Reading & Language Inventory* (7th ed.). New York, NY: Pearson.

Bandura, A. (1977). *Social learning theory*. Englewood Cliffs, NJ: Prentice Hall.

Basaraba, D., Yovanoff, P., Alonzo, J., & Tindal, G. (2013). Examining the structure of reading comprehension: Do literal, inferential, and evaluative comprehension truly exist? *Reading & Writing, 26*(3), 349–379. doi: 10.1007/s11145-012-9372-9

Baumann, J. F., & Kame'enui, E. J. (1991). Research on vocabulary instruction: Ode to Voltaire. In J. Flood, J. J. D. Lapp, & J. R. Squire (Eds.), *Handbook of research on teaching the English language arts* (pp. 604–632). New York, NY: MacMillan.

Baumgartner, T., Lipowski, M. B., & Rush, C. (2003). *Increasing reading achievement of primary and middle school students through differentiated instruction*. Available from Education Resources Information Center (ERIC No. ED79203).

Bear, D. R., Invernizzi, M., Templeton, S., & Johnson, F. (1996). *Words their way: Word study for phonics, vocabulary, and spelling*. Upper Saddle River, NJ: Merrill.

Bear, D. R., Invernizzi, M. Templeton, S., & Johnston, F. (2014). *Words their way: Word study for phonics, vocabulary, and spelling instruction* (5th ed.). Essex, England: Pearson Education Limited.

Beck, I. L., & McKeown, M. G. (2001). Text talk: Capturing the benefits of read-aloud experiences for young children. *The Reading Teacher, 55*(1), 10–20.

References ◆ 215

Beck, I. L., & McKeown, M. G. (2007). Different ways for different goals, but keep your eye on the higher verbal goals. In R. Wagner, A. Muse, & K. Tannenbaum (Eds.), *Vocabulary acquisition: Implications for reading comprehension* (pp. 182–204). New York, NY: Guilford Press.

Beck, I. L., McKeown, M. G., Hamilton, R. L., & Kucan, L. (1997). *Questioning the author: An approach for enhancing student engagement with text*. Newark, DE: International Reading Association.

Beck, I. L., McKeown, M. G., & Kucan, L. (2002). *Bringing words to life: Robust vocabulary instruction*. New York, NY: Guilford.

Becker, W. C. (1977). Teaching reading and language to the disadvantaged: What we have learned from field research. *Harvard Educational Review, 47*, 518–543.

Bell, S. (2010). Project-based learning for the 21st century: Skills for the future. *The Clearing House, 83*, 3–43.

Bender, W. N. (2012). *Project-based learning: Differentiating instruction for the 21st century*. Thousand Oaks, CA: Corwin.

Benson, B. (1997). Scaffolding (Coming to terms). *English Journal, 86*(7), 126–127.

Berninger, V. W. (1999). Coordinating transcription and text generation in working memory during composing: Automatic and constructive processes. *Learning Disability Quarterly, 22*(2), 99–112. doi: 10.2307/1511269

Betts, E. A. (1946). *Foundations of reading instruction: With emphasis on differentiated guidance*. New York, NY: American Book Company.

Biemiller, A. (2001). Teaching vocabulary: Early, direct, and sequential. *American Educator, 25*, 24–28.

Biemiller, A. (2004). Teaching vocabulary in the primary grades. In E. J. Kame'enui & J. F. Baumann (Eds.). *Vocabulary instruction: Research to practice* (pp. 28–40). New York, NY: The Guilford Press.

Biemiller, A., & Slonim, N. (2001). Estimating root word vocabulary growth in normative and advantaged populations: Evidence for a common sequence of vocabulary acquisition. *Journal of Educational Psychology, 93*(3), 498–520.

Bingham, G., Holbrook, T., & Meyers, L. E. (2010). Using self-assessments in elementary classrooms. *Phi Delta Kappan, 91*(5), 59–61. doi: 10.1177/003172171009100515

216 ◆ References

Bitter, C., O'Day, J., Gubbins, P., & Socias, M. (2009). What works to improve student literacy achievement? An examination of instructional practices in a balanced literacy approach. *Journal of Education for Students Placed at Risk, 14*(1), 17–44. doi: 10.1080/10824660802715403

Blachowicz, C.L.Z., & Fisher, P. (2012). Keeping the "fun" in fundamental: Encouraging word consciousness and incidental word learning in the classroom through word play. In E.J. Kame'enui & J.F. Baumann (Eds.). *Vocabulary instruction: Research to practice* (pp. 218–234). New York, NY: The Guilford Press.

Blachowciz, C.L.Z., Fisher, P.J.L., Ogle, D., & Watts-Taffe, S. (2006). Vocabulary: Questions from the classroom. *Reading Research Quarterly, 41*(4), 524–539. doi: 10.1598/RRQ.41.4.5

Blachowicz, C.L.Z., Fisher, P.J., & Watts-Taffe, S. (2005). *Integrated vocabulary instruction: Meeting the needs of diverse learners in Grades K–5*. Naperville, IL: Learning Point Associates.

Block, C. C, & Pressley, M. (Eds.). (2002). *Comprehension instruction: Research-based best practices*. New York, NY: Guilford.

Bloodgood, J.W., & Pacifici, L.C. (2004). Bringing word study to intermediate classrooms. *The Reading Teacher, 58*(3), 240–263. doi: 10:1598/RT.58.3.3

Bloom, B.S. (Ed.). 1956. *Taxonomy of educational objectives: Book 1 cognitive domain*. White Plains, NY: Longman.

Boulware-Gooden, R., Carreker, S., Thornhill, A., & Malatesha Joshi, R. (2007). Instruction of metacognitive strategies enhances reading comprehension and vocabulary achievement of third-grade students. *The Reading Teacher, 61*(1), 70–77. doi: 10.1598/RT.61.1.7

Bowers, P.N., & Kirby, J.R. (2010). Effects of morphological instruction on vocabulary acquisition. *Reading and Writing: An Interdisciplinary Journal, 23*(5), 515–537. doi: 10.1007/s11145-009-9172-z

Boyd-Batstone, P. (2004). Focused anecdotal records assessment: A tool for standards-based authentic assessment. *The Reading Teacher, 58*(3), 230–239. doi: 10.1598/RT.58.3.1

Brabham, E.G., & Lynch-Brown, C. (2002). Effects of teachers' reading-aloud styles on vocabulary acquisition and comprehension of students in the early elementary grades.

Journal of Educational Psychology, 94(3), 465–473. doi: 10.1037/0022-0663.94.3.465

Bromley, K. (2007). Nine things every teacher should know about words and vocabulary instruction. *Journal of Adolescent and Adult Literacy, 50*(7), 528–537. doi: 10.1598/JAAL.50.7.2

Bryant, D. P., Goodwin, M., Bryant, B. R., & Higgins, K. (2003). Vocabulary instruction for students with learning disabilities: A review of the research. *Learning Disability Quarterly, 26*, 117–128.

Buckingham, B. R., & Dolch, E. W. (1936). *A combined word list.* Boston, MA: Ginn.

Burch, J. R. (2007). *A study examining the impact of scaffolding young children's acquisitions of literacy in primary grades* (Doctoral dissertation, Louisiana State University). Retrieved from http://etd.lsu.edu/docs/available/etd-04132007-101339/unrestricted/Burch_dis.pdf.

Burke, L., & Baillie, S. (2011). Literacy centers: A way to increase reading development. *Academic Leadership, 9*(3), 1–8.

Burns, M. K., Kwoka, H., Lim, B., Crone, M., Haegele, K., Parker, D. C., Petersen, S., & Scholin, S. E. (2010). Minimum reading fluency necessary for comprehension among second-grade students. *Psychology in the Schools, 48*(2), 124–132. doi: 10.1002/pits.20531

Cain, K., Lemmon, K., & Oakhill, J. (2004). Individual differences in the inference of word meanings from context: The influence of reading comprehension, vocabulary knowledge, and memory capacity. *Journal of Educational Psychology, 96*(4), 671–681. doi: 10.1037/0022-0663.96.4.671

Campbell, B. (2009). To-with-by: A three-tiered model for differentiated instruction. *The NERA Journal, 44*(2), 7–10.

Campbell, C., & Evans, J. A. (2000). Investigation of preservice teachers' classroom assessment practices during students teaching. *Journal of Educational Research, 93*(6), 350–355.

Carey, S., & Bartlett, E. (1978). Acquiring a single new word. *Proceedings of the Stanford Child Language Conference, 15*, 17–29.

Carlisle, J. F. (2003). Morphology matters in learning to read: A commentary. *Reading Psychology, 24*(3–4), 291–322. doi: 10.1080/02702710390227369

Carlisle, J.F., Stone, C.A., & Katz, L.A. (2001). The effects of phonological transparency on reading derived words. *The Annals of Dyslexia, 51*, 249–274.

Carlo, M.S., August, D., Mclaughlin, B., Snow, C.E., Dressler, C., Lippman, D.N., Lively, T.J., & White. C.E. (2004). Closing the gap: Addressing the vocabulary needs of English-language learners in bilingual and mainstream classrooms. *Reading Research Quarterly, 39*(2), 188–215. doi: 10.1598/RRQ39.2.3

Carnine, D., & Silbert, J. (1979). *Direct instruction reading.* Columbus, OH: Charles Merrill.

Casalis, S., Colé, P., & Sopo, D. (2004). Morphological awareness in developmental dyslexia. *Annals of Dyslexia, 54*, 114–138.

Catherwood, D. (1999). New views on the young brain: Offerings from developmental psychology to early childhood education. *Contemporary Issues in Early Childhood Education, 1*(1), 23–35.

Cauley, K.M., & McMillan, J.H. (2010). Formative assessment techniques to support student motivation and achievement. *The Clearing House, 83*(1), 1–6.

Cazden, C. (1988). *Classroom discourse: The language of teaching and learning.* Portsmouth, NH: Heinemann.

Cazden, C.B., John, V., & Hymes, D. (Eds.). (1972). *Functions of language in the classroom.* New York, NY: Teachers College Press.

Chall, J.S. (1967). *Learning to read: The great debate.* New York, NY: McGraw-Hill.

Chall, J., Jacobs, V. & Baldwin, L. (1990). *The reading crisis: Why poor children fall behind.* Cambridge, MA: Harvard University Press.

Christ, T., & Wang, X.C. (2010). Bridging the vocabulary gap: What the research tells us about vocabulary instruction in early childhood. *Young Children, 65*(4), 84–91.

Cloud, J. (2007, August 16). Are we failing our geniuses? *Time*, 1–4.

Cohen, E., Lotan, R., Scarloss, B., Shultz, S., & Abram, P. (2002). Can groups learn? *Teachers College Record, 104*(6), 1045–1068. doi: 1111/1467-9620.00196

Colangelo, N., Assouline, S.G., & Gross, M.U. (2004). *A nation deceived: How schools hold back America's brightest students* (Vols. 1–2). Iowa City: University of Iowa, The Connie Belin and Jacqueline N. Blank International Center for Gifted Education and Talent Development.

Common Sense Media. (2014). *Children, teens, and reading: A Common Sense Media research brief.* Retrieved from https://www.google.com/#q=common+sense+media+and+pleasure+reading

Cooper, J. D., Warncke, E. W., & Shipman, D. A. (1979). *The what and how of reading instruction.* Columbus, OH: Merrill Publishing Company.

Cowen, J. E. (2003). *A balanced approach to beginning reading instruction: A synthesis of six major U.S. research studies.* Newark, DE: International Reading Association.

Coyne, M. D., Capozzoli-Oldham, A., & Simmons, D. C. (2012). Vocabulary instruction for young children at risk of reading difficulties: Teaching word meanings during shared storybook readings. In E. J. Kame'enui & J. F. Baumann (Eds.). *Vocabulary instruction: Research to practice* (pp. 51–71). New York, NY: The Guilford Press.

Cunningham, A. E., & Stanovich, K. E. (2001). What reading does for the mind. *Journal of Direct Instruction, 1*(2), 137–149.

Cunningham, P., Hall, D., & Cunningham, J. (2000). *Guided reading the four-blocks way.* Greensboro, NC: Carson-Dellosa.

Davis, F. B. (1944). Research in comprehension in reading. *Psychometrika, 9,* 185–197.

Dennis, G., & Walter, E. (1995). The effects of repeated read-alouds on story comprehension as assessed through story retellings. *Reading Improvement, 32*(3), 140–153.

Dewitz, P., Jones, J., & Leahy, S. (2009). Comprehension strategy instruction in core reading programs. *Reading Research Quarterly, 44*(2), 102–126. doi: 10.1598/RRQ.44.2.1

Diehl, H. L., Armitage, C. J., Nettles, D. H., & Peterson, C. (2011). The three-phase reading comprehension intervention (3-RCI): A support for intermediate word callers. *Reading Horizons, 51*(2), 149–170.

Dixon, F. A., Yssel, N., McConnell, J. M., & Hardin, T. (2014). Differentiated instruction, professional development, and teacher efficacy. *Journal for the Education of the Gifted, 37*(2), 111–127. doi: 10.1177/0162353214529042

Dooley, C. M. (2010). Young children's approaches to books: The emergence of comprehension. *The Reading Teacher, 64*(2), 120–130. doi:10.1598/RT.64.2.4.

220 ◆ References

Doppelt, Y. (2003). Implementing and assessment of PBL in a flexible environment. *International Journal of Technology and Design and Design Education, 13*, 255–272.

Dorfman, L., & Cappelli, R. (2007). *Craft lessons: Teaching writing K–8.* Portland, ME: Stenhouse.

Drucker, M.J. (2003). What reading teachers should know about ESL learners. *The Reading Teacher, 57*(1), 22–29.

DuCharme, C., Earl, J., & Poplin, M.S. (1989). The author model: The constructivist view of the writing process. *Learning Disability Quarterly, 12*(3), 237–242.

Duffy, G., Roehler, L., & Mason, J. (Eds.). (1984). *Comprehension instruction: Perspectives and suggestions.* New York, NY: Longman.

Duke, N.K., & Pearson, P.D. (2002). Effective practices for developing reading comprehension. In A.E. Farstup & S.J. Samuels (Eds.), *What research has to say about reading instruction* (pp. 205–242). Newark, DE: International Reading Association.

Durkin, D. (1978/1979). What classroom instruction has to say about reading comprehension instruction. *Reading Research Quarterly, 14*, 481–533.

Durkin, D. (1993). *Teaching them to read* (6th ed.). Boston, MA: Allyn & Bacon.

Eilers, L.H., & Pinkley, C. (2006). Metacognitive strategies help students to comprehend all text. *Reading Improvement, 43*(1), 13–29.

Elbow, P. (2004). Writing first: Putting writing before reading is an effective approach to teaching and learning. *Educational Leadership, 62*(2), 9–13.

Elton, L.R.B., & Laurillard, D.M. (1979). Trends in research on student learning. *Studies in Higher Education, 4*(1), 87–102.

Feldhusen, J.F. (1992). Grouping gifted students: Issues and concerns. *Gifted Child Quarterly, 36*(2), 63–67.

Fisher, C.W., & Hiebert, E.H. (1990). Characteristics of tasks in two approaches to literacy instruction. *The Elementary School Journal, 91*(1), 3–18.

Fisher, D., Flood, J., Lapp, D., & Frey, N. (2004). Interactive read alouds: Is there a common set of implementation practices. *The Reading Teacher, 58*(1), 8–17. doi: 10.1598/RT.58.1.1

References ◆ 221

Fisher, D., & Frey, N. (2008). What does it take to create skilled readers? Facilitating the transfer and application of literacy strategies. *Voices from the Middle, 15*(4), 16–22.

Flanders, N. (1970). *Analyzing teacher behavior*. Reading, MA: Addison-Wesley.

Flesch, R. (1955, 1986). *Why Johnny can't read and what you can do about it*. New York, NY: Harper & Brothers.

Fletcher, J. F., Greenwood, J., Grimley, M., Parkhill, F., & Davis, N. (2012). What is happening when teachers of 11–13-year-old students take guided reading: A New Zealand snapshot. *Educational Review, 64*(4), 425–449. doi: 10.1080/00131911.2.00.625112 10.1080/00131911.2011.625112

Flood, J., Lapp, D., & Fisher, D. (2005). Neurological impress method plus. *Reading Psychology: An International Quarterly, 26*, 147–160.

Ford, M. P., & Opitz, M. F. (2002). Using centers to engage children during guided reading time: Intensifying learning experiences away from the teacher. *The Reading Teacher, 55*(8), 710–717.

Ford, M. P., & Opitz, M. F. (2011). Looking back to move forward with guided reading. *Reading Horizons, 50*(4), 225–240.

Fordham, N. W., Wellman, D., & Sandmann, A. (2002). Taming the text: Engaging and supporting students in social studies readings. *The Social Studies, 93*, 149–158.

Fountas, I., & Pinnell, G. (1996). *Guided reading: Good first teaching for all children*. Portsmouth, NH: Heinemann.

Fountas, I. C., & Pinnell, G. S. (2012). Guided reading: The romance and the reality. *The Reading Teacher, 66*(4), 268–284. doi:10.1002/ TRTR.01123

French, C., Morgan, J., Vanayan, M., & White, N. (2001). Balanced literacy: Implementation and evaluation. *Education Canada, 40*(4), 23.

Fry, E. B., Kress, J. E., & Fountoukidis, D. L. (2000). *The reading teacher's book of lists* (4th ed.). Paramus, NJ: Prentice Hall.

Fuchs, D., & Fuchs, L. (2005). Peer-assisted learning strategies: Promoting word recognition, fluency, and reading comprehension in young children. *Journal of Special Education, 39*, 34–44.

Fuchs, L. S., Fuchs, D., Hosp, M. K., & Jenkins, J. R. (2001). Oral reading fluency as an indicator of reading competence: A theoretical, empirical, and historical analysis. *Scientific Studies of Reading, 5*, 239–256.

Gallagher, K. (2011). *Write like this: Teaching real-world writing through modeling and mentor texts*. Portland, ME: Stenhouse.

Gambrell, L., Block, C. C., & Pressley, M. (2002). *Improving comprehension instruction*. Newark, NJ: Jossey-Bass.

Garan, E. M., & DeVoogd, G. (2008). The benefits of sustained silent reading: Scientific research and common sense converge. *The Reading Teacher, 62*(4), 336–344. doi: 10.1598/RT.62.4.6

Gibson, S. A. (2008). Guided writing lessons: Second-grade students' development of strategic behavior. *Reading Horizons, 48*(2), 111–132.

Gilbert, J., & Graham, S. (2010). Teaching writing to elementary students in Grades 4–6: A national survey. *The Elementary School Journal, 110*(4), 494–518.

Graham, S., Harris, K. R., & Fink-Chorzempa, B. (2002). Contributions of spelling instruction to the spelling, writing, and reading of poor spellers. *Journal of Educational Psychology, 94*, 291–304.

Graham, S., Harris, K. R., Fink-Chorzempa, B., & MacArthur, C. (2003). Primary grade teachers' instructional adaptations for struggling writers: A national survey. *Journal of Educational Psychology, 95*(2), 279–292. doi: 10.1037/0022–0663.95.2.279

Graham, S., & Hebert, M. (2010). *Writing to read: Evidence for how writing can improve reading*. Washington, DC: Alliance of Excellence in Education.

Graham, S., & Perrin, D. (2007a). What we know, what we still need to know: Teaching adolescents to write. *Scientific Studies in Reading, 11*, 313–336.

Graham, S., & Perrin, D. (2007b). *Writing next: Effective strategies to improve writing of adolescents in middle and high school*. Washington, DC: Alliance for Excellent Education.

Graves, M. F. (2009). *Teaching individual words: One size does not fit all*. Newark: DE: International Reading Association.

Graves, M. F., Baumann, J. F., Blachowicz, C. L. Z., Manyak, P., Bates, A., Cieply, C., Davis, J. R., & Von Gunten, H. (2014). Words, words everywhere, but which ones do we teach? *The Reading Teacher, 67*(5), 333–346. doi: 10.1002/TRTR.1228

Graves, M. F., & Fitzgerald, J. (2003). Scaffolding reading experiences for multilingual classrooms. In Gilbert G. Garcia (Ed.), *English language learners: Reaching the highest level of English literacy* (pp. 96–124). Newark, DE: International Reading Association.

Gray, L., & Reese, D. (1957). *Teaching children to read.* New York: The Ronald Press Company.

Green, T. M. (2008). *The Greek and Latin roots of English* (4th ed.). Lanham, MD: Rowman & Littlefield Publishers.

Griffith, L. W., & Rasinski, T. V. (2004). A focus on literacy: How one teacher incorporated fluency with her reading curriculum. *The Reading Teacher, 58*(2), 126–137. doi: 10.1598/RT.58.2.1

Gruber, G. (1986). *Essential guide to test taking for kids, Grades 3, 4, & 5.* New York, NY: Collins.

Hall, B. W., & Hewitt-Gervais, C. H. (2000). The application of student portfolios in primary-intermediate and self-contained-multiage team classroom environments: Implications for instruction, learning, and assessment. *Applied Measurement in Education, 13*(2), 209–228.

Harris, T., & Hodges, R. (1995). *The literacy dictionary: The vocabulary of reading and writing.* Newark, DE: International Reading Association.

Harvey, S., & Goudvis, A. (2000). *Strategies that work.* Markham, Ontario, Canada: Pembroke.

Heacox, D. (2002). *Differentiating instruction in the regular classroom: How to reach and teach all learners, Grades 3–12.* Minneapolis, MN: Free Spirit Publishing.

Heacox, D. (2009). *Making differentiation a habit: How to ensure success in academically diverse classrooms.* Minneapolis, MN: Free Spirit Publishing.

Hiebert, E. H. (2005). In pursuit of an effective, efficient vocabulary curriculum for elementary students. In E. H. Hiebert & M. L. Kamil (Eds.), *Teaching and learning vocabulary: Bringing research to practice* (pp. 243–363). Mahwah, NJ: Erlbaum.

Hirsch, E. D. (2003, Spring). Reading comprehension requires knowledge—of words and the world: Scientific insights into the fourth-grade slump and the nation's stagnant comprehension scores. *American Educator, 10*(13), 16–29.

224 ◆ References

Hoetker, J., & Ahlbrand, W. Jr. (1969). The persistence of the recitation. *American Education Research Journal, 6*, 145–167.

Hoffman, J.V., Roser, N.L., & Battle, J. (1993). Reading aloud in classrooms: From the model toward a "model." *The Reading Teacher, 46*(6), 496–503.

Hogan, T.P., Catts, H.W., & Little, T.D. (2005). The relationship between phonological awareness and reading: Implications for the assessment of phonological awareness. *Language Speech and Hearing Services in Schools, 36*(4), 285–293.

Holdaway, D. (1979). *The foundations of literacy.* New York, NY: Ashton Scholastic.

Hollingworth, L.S. (1922). Provisions for intellectually superior children. In M.V. O'Shea (Ed.), *The child, his nature, and his needs* (pp. 10–32). New York, NY: Arno Press.

Hoogeveen, M., & van Gelderen, A. (2013). What works in writing with peer response? A review of intervention studies with children and adolescents. *Educational Psychology Review, 25*, 473–502. doi: 10.1007/s10648-013-9229-z

Huey, E.B. (1968). *The psychology and pedagogy of reading.* Cambridge, MA: MIT Press. (Originally published 1908).

Huff, J.D., & Nietfield, J.L. (2009). Using strategy instruction and confidence judgments to improve metacognitive monitoring. *Metacognitive Learning, 4*, 161–176. doi: 10.1007/s11409-009 -9042-8

Hunt, L.C., Jr. (1984). Six steps to the individualized reading program (IRP). In A.J. Harris & E.R. Sipay (Eds.), *Readings on reading instruction* (pp. 190–195). New York, NY: Longman.

International Reading Association. (1999). *Adolescent literacy: A position statement.* [Brochure]. Newark, DE: Author.

Invernizz, M., & Hayes, L. (2004). Developmental-spelling research: A systematic imperative. *Reading Research Quarterly, 39*(2), 216–228. doi: 10.1598/RRQ.39.2.4

Isbell, R., Sobol, J., Lindauer, L., & Lowrance, A. (2004). The effects of a storytelling and story reading on the oral language complexity and story comprehension of young children. *Early Childhood Education Journal, 32*(3), 157–163.

Ivey, G., & Broaddus, K. (2001). Just plain reading: A survey of what makes students want to read in middle school classrooms.

Reading Research Quarterly, 36(4), 350–377. doi: 10.1598/ RRQ.36.4.2

James, K.H. (2012, January 23). "How Printing Practice Affects Letter Perception: An Educational Cognitive Neuroscience Perspective." Presented at Handwriting in the 21st Century: An Educational Summit, Washington, DC.

January, S.A., & Ardoin, S.P. (2012). The impact of context and word type on students' maze task accuracy. *School Psychology Review, 41*(3), 262–271.

Johns, J. L. (2010). *Basic Reading Inventory* (10th ed.). Dubuque, IA: Kendall Hunt Publishing Company.

Johnston, F.R. (2001). Exploring classroom teachers' spelling practices and beliefs. *Reading Research and Instruction, 40*(2), 143–156.

Jones, D., & Christensen, C. (1999). The relationship between automaticity in handwriting and students' ability to generate written text. *Journal of Educational Psychology, 91*, 44–49.

Juel, C. (1988). Learning to read and write: A longitudinal study of 54 children from first through fourth grades. *Journal of Educational Psychology, 78*, 243–255.

Kaldi, S., Filippatou, D., & Govaris, C. (2011). Project-based learning in primary schools: Effects on learning and attitudes. *Education, 39*(1), 35–47.

Kanter, R.M. (2006). *Confidence: How winning streaks losing streaks begin and end*. New York, NY: Random House.

Keene, E., & Zimmerman, S. (1997). *Mosaic of thought: Teaching comprehension in a reader's workshop*. Portsmouth, NH: Heinemann.

Keene, E.O., & Zimmerman, S. (2013). Years later, comprehension strategies still at work. *The Reading Teacher, 66*(8), 601–606. doi: 10.1002/TRTR.1167

Kelley, J.G., Lesaux, N.K., Kieffer, M.J., & Faller, S.E. (2010). Effective academic vocabulary instruction in the urban middle school. *The Reading Teacher, 64*(1), 5–14. doi: 10.1598/RT.64.1.1

Kelley, M.J., & Clausen-Grace, N. (2009). Facilitating engagement by differentiating independent reading. *The Reading Teacher, 63*(4), 313–318. doi: 10.1598/RT.63.4.6

Ketch, A. (2005). Conversation: The comprehension connection. *The Reading Teacher, 59*(1), 8–13. doi: 10.1598/RT.59.1.2

Kieffer, M.J., & Lesaux, N. K. (2008). The role of derivational morphology in the reading comprehension of Spanish-speaking English Language Learners. *Reading and Writing: An Interdisciplinary Journal, 21*(8), 783–804. doi: 10.1007/s11145-007-9092-8

Kim, C. (2013). Vocabulary acquisition with affixation: Learning English words based on prefixes and suffixes. *Second Language Studies, 31*(2), 43–80.

Kirby, J.R., Deacon, S.H., Bowers, P.N., Izenberg, L., Wade-Woolley, L., & Parrila, R. (2012). Children's morphological awareness and reading ability. *Reading and Writing: An Interdisciplinary Journal, 25*, 389–410. doi: 10.1007/s11145–010–9276–5

Kirk, C., & Gillon, G.T. (2009). Integrated morphological awareness intervention as a tool for improving literacy. *Language, Speech, and Hearing Services in School, 40*(3), 341–351. doi: 0161 –1461/09/4003–0341

Kirschenbaum, R.J. (1995). An interview with Dr. Joseph Renzulli and Dr. Sally Reis. *Gifted Child Today, 18*(4), 18–21, 24–25.

Klassen, R. (2002). Writing in early adolescence: A review of the role of self-efficacy beliefs. *Educational Psychology Review, 14*(2), 173–203.

Klingner, J.K., Urbach, J., Golos, D., Brownell, M., & Menon, S. (2010). Teaching reading in the 21st century: A glimpse at how special education teachers promote reading comprehension. *Learning Disability Quarterly, 33*, 59–74.

Knudson, R.E. (1995). Writing experiences, attitudes, and achievement of first to sixth graders. *The Journal of Educational Research, 89*(2), 90–97.

Koskinen, P.S., Blum, I.H., Bisson, S. A, Phillips, S.M., Creamer, T.S., & Baker, T.K. (1999). Shared reading, books, and audiotapes: Supporting diverse students in school and at home. *The Reading Teacher, 52*(5), 430–444.

Kragler, S., Walker, C.A., & Martin, L.E. (2005). Strategy instruction in primary content textbooks. *The Reading Teacher, 59*(3), 254–261. doi: 10.1598/RT.59.3.5

Krashen, S.D. (2004). *Power of reading: Insights from the research.* Portsmouth, NH: Heinemann.

Kuhn, M., Schwanenflugel, P., & Meisinger, E. (2010). Aligning theory and assessment of reading fluency: Automaticity, prosody, and definitions of fluency. *Reading Research Quarterly, 45*(2), 230–251. doi: 10.1598/RRQ.45.2.4

Kuhn, M. R., & Rasinski, T. V. (2015). Best practices in fluency instruction. In L. B. Gambrell & L. M. Morrow (Eds.), *Best practices in literacy instruction* (pp. 268–287). New York, NY: The Guilford Press.

Kühnen, U., van Egmond, M. C., Haber, F., Kuschel, S., Özelsel, A., Rossi, A. L., & Spivak, Y. (2012). Challenge me! Communicating in multicultural classrooms. *Social Psychology of Education, 15*(1), 59–76.

Kuo, L. J., & Anderson, R. C. (2006). Morphological awareness and learning to read: A cross-language perspective. *Educational Psychologist, 41*(3), 161–180. doi: 10.1207/s15326985ep4103_3

LaBerge, D., & Samuels, S. J. (1974). Toward a theory of automatic information processing in reading. *Cognitive Psychology, 6*, 293–323. doi: 10.1016/0010–0285(74)90015–2

Lapp, D., & Fisher, D. (2009). It's all about the book: Motivating teens to read. *Journal of Adolescent Adult Literacy, 52*(7), 556–561. doi: 10.1598/JAAL.52.7.1

LaPray, M., & Ross, R. (1969). The graded word list: Quick gauge of reading ability. *Journal of Reading, 12*, 305–307.

Larmer, J., & Mergendoller, J. R. (2010). 7 essentials for project-based learning. *Educational Leadership, 68*(1), 34–37.

Laud, L., Hirsch, S., Patel, P., & Wagner, M. (2010). Maximize student achievement with formative assessment. *ASCD Express, 6*(1). Retrieved from http://www.ascd.org/ascd-express/vol6/601laud.aspx

Lee, I. (2011). Working smarter, not working harder: Revisiting teacher feedback in the L2 writing classroom. *The Canadian Modern Language Review, 67*(3), 377–399. doi: 10.3138/cmlr.67.3.377

Lesaux, N. K., & Kieffer, M. J. (2010). Exploring sources of reading comprehension difficulties among language minority learners and their classmates in early adolescence. *American Educational Research Journal, 47*(3), 596–632. doi: 10.3102/0002831209355469

Leslie, L., & Caldwell, J. S. (2011). *Qualitative Reading Inventory* (5th ed.). New York, NY: Pearson.

Leven, T., & Long, R. (1981). *Effective instruction*. Washington, DC: ASCD.

Levy, B.A., Gong, Z., Hessels, S., Evans, M., & Jared, D. (2006). Understanding print: Early reading development and the contributions of home literacy experiences. *Journal of Experimental Child Psychology, 93*(1), 63–93.

Licht, M. (2014). Controlled chaos: Project-based learning. *The Education Digest, 80*(2), 49–51.

Linn, R.L. (2000). Assessments and accountability. *Educational Researcher, 29*(2), 4–16.

Lipson, M.Y., Mosenthal, J.H., Mekkelsen, J., & Russ, B. (2004). Building knowledge and fashioning success one school at a time. *The Reading Teacher, 57*(6), 534–542. doi: 10.1598/RT.57.6.3

Lyon, G.R. (1995). Toward a definition of dyslexia. *Annals of Dyslexia, 45*, 3–27.

MacDonald, G.W., & Cornwall, A. (1995). *The relationship between phonological awareness* and reading and spelling achievement eleven years later. *Journal of Learning Disabilities, 28*(8), 523–527.

MacKenzie, N., & Hemmings, B. (2014). Predictors of success with writing in the first year of school. *Issues in Educational Research, 24*(1), 41–54.

Mahoney, D. (1994). Using sensitivity to word structure to explain variance in high school and college level reading ability. *Reading and Writing: An Interdisciplinary Journal, 6*, 19–44.

Mann, V.A., & Singson, M. (2003). The little suffix that could: Linking morphological knowledge to English decoding ability. In E. Assink & D. Sandra (Eds.), *Morphology and reading: A cross-linguistic perspective* (pp. x–xx). Amsterdam, The Netherlands: Kluver Publishers.

Marland, S.P. Jr. (1972). *Education of the gifted and talented: Report to the Congress of the United States by the U.S. Commissioner of Education*. Washington, DC: U.S. Government Printing Office.

Maurer, C. (2010). Meeting academic standards through peer dialogue at literacy centers. *Language Arts, 87*(5), 353–362.

McBride-Chang, C., Wagner, R.K., Muse, A., Chow, B.W., & Shu, H. (2005). The role of morphological awareness in children's vocabulary acquisition in English. *Applied Psycholinguistics, 26*, 415–435.

McKeown, M., Beck, I., Omanson, R., & Pople, M. (1985). Some effects of the nature and frequency of vocabulary instruction on the knowledge and use of words. *Reading Research Quarterly, 20*(5), 522–535.

McKeown, M.G., Beck, I.L., & Sandora, S. (2012). Direct and rich vocabulary instruction needs to start early in E.J. Kame'enui & J.F. Baumann, (Eds.), *Vocabulary instruction: Research to practice.* New York, NY: The Guilford Press.

McGill-Franzen, A., Zmach, C., Solic, K., & Zeig, J.L. (2006). The confluence of two policy mandates: Core reading programs and third grade retention in Florida. *Elementary School Journal, 107*, 67–91.

McMahan, G.A., & Gifford, A.P. (2001). Portfolio: Achieving your personal best. *The Delta Kappa Gamma Bulletin, 68*(1), 36–41.

McQuarrie, L., McRae, P., & Stack-Cutler, H. (2008). *Differentiated instruction provincial research review.* Edmonton, Canada: Alberta Initiative for School Improvement.

Mergendoller, J.R., Maxwell, N.L., & Bellisimo, Y. (2006). The effectiveness of problem-based instruction: A comparative study of instructional methods and student characteristics. *The Interdisciplinary Journal of Problem-Based Learning, 1*(2), 46–69.

Meyer, L.A., Stahl, S.A., Linn, R.L., & Wardrop, J.L. (2001). Effects of reading storybooks aloud to children. *Journal of Educational Research, 88*(2), 69–85.

Mody, M. (2003). Phonological basis in reading disability: A review and analysis of evidence. *Reading and Writing: An Interdisciplinary Journal, 16*, 21–39.

Mooney, M.E. (1990). *Reading TO, WITH, and BY children.* Katonah, NY: Richard C. Owens Publishers, Inc.

Morgan, D.N., Mraz, M., Padak, N., & Rasinski, T. (2009). *Independent reading: Practical strategies for Grades K–3.* New York, NY: Guilford.

Nagy, W.E. (2005). Why vocabulary instruction needs to be long-term and comprehensive. In E.H. Hiebert & M.L. Kamil (Eds.), *Teaching and learning vocabulary: Bringing research into practice* (pp. 27–44). Mahwah, NJ: Erlbaum.

Nagy, W.E., & Anderson, R.C. (1984). How many words are there in printed school English? *Reading Research Quarterly, 19*(3), 304–330.

Nagy, W.E., & Anderson, R.C., & Herman, P.A. (1987). Learning word meanings from context during normal reading. *American Educational Research Journal, 24*(2), 237–270.

Nagy, W. E., Berninger, V. W., & Abbott, R. B. (2006). Contributions of morphology beyond phonology to literacy outcomes of upper elementary and middle-school students. *Journal of Educational Psychology, 98*(1), 134–147.

Nagy, W. E., & Scott, J. A. (2000). *Vocabulary processes*. In M. L. Kamil, P. B. Mosenthal, P. D. Pearson, and R. Barr (Eds.), *Handbook of reading research* (Vol. 3, pp. 269–284). Mahwah, NJ: Lawrence Erlbaum.

National Commission on Writing America's Schools and Colleges. (2003). *The neglected "R": The need for a writing revolution*. Retrieved from http://www.collegeboard.com/prod_downloads/writingcom/neglectedr.pdf

National Endowment for the Arts. (2007). *To read or not to read: A question of national consequence*. Research Report no. 47. Washington, DC: Authors.

National Reading Council. (1998). *Preventing reading difficulties in young children*. National Academy Press.

National Reading Panel. (2000). *Report of the National Reading Panel: Teaching children to read*. Washington, DC: National Institute of Child Health and Human Development.

NCES. (2003). *The Nation's report card: Writing 2002* (NCES 2003–529) By H. R. Persky, M. C. Dane, & Y. Jin. Washington, DC.

Ness, M. K. (2009). Reading comprehension strategies in secondary area content classrooms: Teacher use of and attitudes toward reading comprehension instruction. *Reading Horizons, 49*(2), 143–166.

Pacheco, M. B., & Goodwin, A. P. (2013). Putting two and two together: Middle school students' morphological problem-solving strategies for unknown words. *Journal of Adolescent and Adult Literacy, 56*(7), 541–553. doi: 10.1002/JAAL.181

Palinscar, A., & Brown, A. (1983). *A reciprocal teaching of comprehension-monitoring activities*. (Technical Report No. 269). Urbana, IL: University of Illinois, Center for the Study of Reading.

Palincsar, A. S., & Brown, A. L. (1989). Classroom dialogues to promote self-regulated comprehension. In S. Brophy (Ed.), *Teaching for understanding and self-regulated learning* (Vol. 1, pp. 35–67). Greenwich, CT: JAI Press.

Pearson, P.D., & Gallagher, M.C. (1983). The instruction of reading comprehension. *Contemporary Educational Psychology, 8,* 317–344.

Phillips, S. (2008). Are we holding back our students that possess the potential to excel? *Education, 129*(1), 50–55.

Piaget, J. (1952). *The origins of intelligence in children.* New York, NY: International Universities Press.

Plake, B.S. (1993). Teacher assessment literacy: Teachers' competencies in the educational assessment of students. *Mid-Western Educational Researcher, 61*(1), 21–27.

Postlethwaite, T.N., & Ross, K.N. (1992). *Effective schools in reading: Implications for educational planners.* Hague, The Netherlands: International Association for the Evaluation of Educational Achievement.

Powell, G. (1980). A meta-analysis of the effects of "imposed" and "induced" imagery upon word recall. Paper presented at the annual meeting of the National Reading Conference, San Diego, CA. (ERIC No. ED199644)

Powell, W.R. (1986). Teaching vocabulary through opposition. *Journal of Reading, 29,* 617–621.

Pressley, M. (2006, April 29). *What the future of reading research could be.* Paper presented at the International Reading Association Reading Research Conference, Chicago, IL.

Pressley, M., Wharton-McDonald, R., Allington, R., Block, C., Morrow, L., Tracey, D., Baker, K., Brooks, G., Cronin, J., Nelson, E., & Woo, D. (2001). Strategy instruction for elementary students searching informational text. *Scientific Studies of Reading, 5,* 35–59.

Qian, D.D. (1999). Assessing the roles of depth and breadth of vocabulary knowledge in reading comprehension. *The Canadian Modern Language Review, 56*(2), 282–306.

Quirk, M., & Beem, S. (2012). Examining the relations between reading fluency and reading comprehension for English language learners. *Psychology in the Schools, 49*(6), 539–553. doi: 10.1002/pits.21616

RAND Reading Study Group. (2002). *Reading for understanding: Toward an R & D program in reading comprehension.* Santa Monica, CA: RAND.

232 ◆ References

Rasinski, T.V. (1990). *The effects of cued phrase boundaries on reading performance: A review.* Kent, OH: Kent State University. (ERIC Document Reproduction Service No. ED313689).

Rasinski, T.V. (1994). Developing syntactic sensitivity in reading through phrase-cued texts. *Intervention in School and Clinic, 29*(3), 165–168.

Rasinski, T. (2004). Creating fluent readers. *Educational Leadership, 61*(6), 46–51.

Reading, S., & Van Deuren, D. (2007). Phonemic awareness: When and how much to teach? *Reading Research and Instruction, 46*(3), 267–286. doi: 10.1080/19388070709558471

Reinhartz, J. (1986). *Teach-practice-apply: The TPA instruction model, K–8.* Retrieved from ERIC database. (ED278662).

Reis, S.M., Eckert, R.D., McCoach, D.B., Jacobs, J.K., & Coyne, M. (2008). Using enrichment reading practices to increase reading fluency, comprehension, and attitudes. *The Journal of Educational Research, 101*(5), 299–314. doi: 10.3200/JOER.101.5

Reis, S., & Renzulli, J. (1992). Using curriculum compacting to challenge the above average. *Educational Leadership, 50*(2), 51–57.

Reutzel, D.R., Jones, C.D., & Newman, T.H. (2010). Scaffolded silent reading: Improving the practice of silent reading practice in classrooms. In E.H. Hiebert & D.R. Reutzel (Eds.), *Revisiting silent reading: New directions for teachers and researchers* (pp. 129–150). Newark, DE: International Reading Association.

Ritchey, K.D. (2008). The building blocks of writing: Learning to write letters and spell words. *Reading and Writing: An Interdisciplinary Journal, 21*, 27–47. doi: 10.1007/s11145–007–9063–0

Rivard, L.P., & Straw, S.B. (2000). The effect of talk and writing on learning science: An exploratory study. *Science Education, 84*(5), 566–593.

Robb, L. (2000). *Teaching reading in middle school: A strategic approach to teaching reading that improves comprehension and thinking.* New York, NY: Scholastic Professional Books.

Rock, M., Gregg, M., Ellis, E., & Gable, R.A. (2008). REACH: A framework for differentiating classroom instruction. *Preventing School Failure, 52*(2), 31–47.

Roser, N., & Juel, C. (1982). Effect of vocabulary instruction on reading comprehension. In J.A. Niles & L.A. Harris (Eds.), *New inquiries in reading research: Research and instruction: Thirty-first yearbook of*

the National Reading Convention (Vol. 31, pp. 110–118).
Rochester, NY: National Reading Conference.

Roskos, K. (2004). Early literacy assessment—Thoughtful, sensible, and good. *The Reading Teacher, 58*(1), 91–94.

Roskos, K., & Neuman, S.B. (2012). Formative assessment: Simply, no additives. *The Reading Teacher, 65*(8), 534–538. doi: 10.1002/TRTR.01079

Routman, R. (2000). *Conversations: Strategies for teaching, learning, and evaluating*. Portsmouth, NH: Heinemann.

Rupley, W.H. (2005). Vocabulary knowledge: Its contribution to reading growth and development. *Reading & Writing Quarterly, 21*, 203–207. doi: 10.1080/10573560590949179

Safadi, E., & Rababah, G. (2012). The effect of scaffolding instruction on reading comprehension skills. *International Journal of Language Studies, 6*(2), 1–38.

Samuels, S.J. (1979). The method of repeated readings. *The Reading Teacher, 23*(4), 403–408.

Samuels, S.J. (1988). Decoding and automaticity. *The Reading Teacher, 41*(8), 756–760.

Samuels, S.J. (2012). Reading fluency: Its past, present, and future. In T. Raskinski, C. Blachowicz, & K. Lems (Eds.), *Fluency instruction: Research-based best practices* (pp. 3–16). New York, NY: The Guilford Press.

Santoro, L.E., Chard, D.J., Howard, L., & Baker, S.K. (2008). Making the very most of classroom read-alouds to promote comprehension and vocabulary. *The Reading Teacher, 61*(5), 396–408. doi: 10.1598/RT.61.5.4

Schisler, R., Joseph, L.M., Konrad, M., & Alber-Morgan, S. (2010). Comparison of the effectiveness and efficiency of oral and written retellings and passage review as strategies for comprehending text. *Psychology in the Schools, 47*(2), 135–152. doi: 10.1002/pits.20460

Scott, J.A., & Nagy, W.E. (1997). Understanding the definitions of unfamiliar verbs. *Reading Research Quarterly, 32*(2), 184–200.

Serafini, F., & Giorgis, C. (2003). *Reading aloud and beyond*. Portsmouth, NH: Heinemann.

Shanahan, T. (2006). *The National Reading Panel Report: Practical advice for teachers*. Naperville, IL: Learning Point Associates.

234 ◆ References

Shannon, P. (1989). *Broken promises: Reading instruction in twentieth-century America.* Granby, MA: Bergin & Garvey.

Simons, K. D., & Klein, J. D. (2007). The impact of scaffolding and student achievement levels in a problem-based learning environment. *Instructional Science, 35*(1), 41–72.

Simpson, C. G., Spencer, V. G., Button, R., & Rendon, S. (2007). Using guided reading with students with autism spectrum disorders. *Teaching Exceptional Children Plus, 4*(1), Article 5. Retrieved from http://files.eric.ed.gov/fulltext/EJ967470.pdf

Smith, N. B. (2002). *American reading instruction.* Newark, DE: International Reading Association. (Original work published in 1934).

Snow, C. E., Burns, M. S., & Griffin, P. (1998). *Preventing reading difficulties in young children.* Washington, DC: National Academy Press.

Snyder, L. G., & Snyder, M. J. (2008). Teaching critical thinking and problem-solving skills. *The Delta Pi Epsilon Journal, 50*(2), 90–99.

Sobolak, M. J. (2011). Modifying robust vocabulary instruction for the benefit of low-socioeconomic students. *Reading Improvement, 48*(1), 14–23.

Stahl, K. A. D. (2004). Proof, practice, and promise: Comprehension strategy instruction in the primary grades. *Reading Teacher, 57*(7), 598–609.

Stahl, S. A. (2004). Vocabulary learning and the child with learning disabilities. *Perspectives, 30*, 1.

Stahl, S. A., & Nagy, W. E. (2006). *Teaching word meanings.* Mahwah, NJ: Erlbaum.

Stamps, L. S. (2004). The effectiveness of curriculum compacting in first grade classrooms. *Roeper Review, 27*(1), 31–41.

Stanovich, K. E. (1986). Matthew effects in reading: Some consequences in individual differences in the acquisition of literacy. *Reading Research Quarterly, 21*, 360–407. doi: 10.1598/RRQ.21.4.1

Stanovich, K. E. (1994). Romance and reality. *The Reading Teacher, 47*(4), 280–291.

Stiggins, R. J. (1999). Are you assessment literate? *The High School Journal, 6*(5), 20–23.

Stiggins, R. (2009). Assessment for learning in upper elementary grades. *Phi Delta Kappan, 90*(6), 419–421. doi: 10.1177/003172170909000608

References ◆ 235

Storch, S.A., & Whitehurst, G.J. (2002). Oral language and code-related precursors to reading: Evidence from a longitudinal structural model. *Development Psychology, 38*, 937–947.

Sudweeks, R.R., Glissmeyer, C.B., Morrison, T.G., Wilcox, B.R., & Tanner, M.W. (2004). Establishing reliable procedures for rating ELL students' reading comprehension using oral retellings. *Reading Research and Instruction, 43*(2), 65–86.

Suits, B. (2003). Guided reading and second-language learners. *Multicultural Education, 11*(2), 27–34.

Systematic Instruction and the Project Approach. (n.d.). *Projectapproach. org.* Retrieved from http://projectapproach.org/special-topics/ systematic-instruction/

Tamin, S.R., & Grant, M.M. (2013). Definitions and uses: Case study of teachers implementing project-based learning. *Interdisciplinary Journal of Problem-Based Learning, 7*(2), 72–101. doi: 10.7771/1541-5015.1323

Taylor, B.M., Pearson, P.D., Clark, K.F., & Walpole, S. (2000). Effective schools and accomplished teachers: Lessons about primary-grade reading instruction in low-income schools. *Elementary School Journal, 101*, 121–164.

Templeton, S. (2011/2012). Teaching and learning morphology: A reflection on generative vocabulary instruction. *Journal of Education, 192*(2–3), 101–107.

Templeton, S. (2012). The vocabulary-spelling connection and generative instruction: Orthographic development and morphological knowledge at the intermediate grades and beyond. In E.J. Kame'enui & J.F. Baumann (Eds.). *Vocabulary instruction: Research to practice* (pp. 118–138). New York, NY: The Guilford Press.

Therrien, W.J. (2004). Fluency and comprehension gains as a result of repeated reading: A meta-analysis. *Remedial and Special Education, 25*(4), 252–261. doi: 10.1177/07419325040250040801

Tomlinson, C.A. (1999). *The differentiated classroom: Responding to the needs of all learners.* Alexandria, VA: ASCD.

Tomlinson, C.A. (2001). *How to differentiate in mixed-ability classrooms.* Alexandria, VA: ASCD.

Tomlinson, C.A. (2009). Intersections between differentiation and literacy instruction: Shared principles worth sharing. *The NERA Journal, 45*(1), 28–33.

Tong, X., Deacon, S. H., Kirby, J. R., Cain, K., & Parrila, R. (2011). Morphological awareness: A key to understanding poor reading comprehension in English. *Journal of Educational Psychology, 103*(3), 523–534. doi: 10.1037/a0023495

Torgesen, J. K. (2002). The prevention of reading difficulties. *Journal of School Psychology, 40*, 7–26.

Torgesen, J. K. (2004). Lessons learned from research on interventions for students who have difficulty learning to read. In P. McCardle & V. Chhabra (Eds.), *The voice of evidence in reading research* (pp. 355–382). Baltimore, MD: Paul H. Brookes.

U.S. Department of Education. (1993). *National excellence: A case for developing America's talent.* (ERIC No. ED359743)

Vadasy, P. F., & Nelson, J. R. (2012). *Vocabulary instruction for struggling students.* New York, NY: The Guilford Press.

Van Keer, H. (2004). Fostering reading comprehension in fifth grade by explicit instruction in reading strategies and peer tutoring. *British Journal of Educational Psychology, 74*, 37–70.

Van de Pol, J., Volman, M., & Beishuizen, J. (2010). Scaffolding in teacher-student interaction: A decade of research. *Educational Psychology Review, 22*(3), 271–296. doi: 10.1007/s10648 –010–9127–6

Vaughn, S., Moody, S., & Schumm, J. S. (1998). Broken promises: Reading instruction in the resource room. *Exceptional Children, 64*(2), 211–226.

Venezky, R. (1987). Steps toward a modern history of American reading instruction. *Review of Research in Education, 13*, 129–167.

Vygotsky, L. S. (1962). *Thought and language.* Cambridge, MA: MIT Press. (Original work published in 1934).

Vygotsky, L. S. (1978). *Mind in society: The development of higher psychological processes.* Cambridge, MA: Harvard University Press.

Wallis, C., & Steptoe, S. (2006, December 18). How to bring our schools out of the 20th century. *Time, 168*(25), 50–56.

Webb, N. L. (1997). *Criteria for alignment of expectations and assessments in mathematics and science education.* Council of Chief State School Officers an National Institute for Science Education Research Monograph No. 8. Madison, WI: University of Wisconsin, Wisconsin Center for Education Research.

Webb, N. L. (1999). *Research monograph No. 18. Alignment of science and mathematics standards and assessments in four states.* Washington, DC: Council of Chief State School Officers.

Weber, W. R., & Henderson, E. H. (1989). A computer-based program of word study: Effects on reading and spelling. *Reading Psychology, 10*, 157–171.

Welsch, R. G. (2006). 20 ways to increase oral reading fluency. *Intervention in School and Clinic, 41*(3), 180–183.

Wilkinson, E. R., & Silliman, L. C. (2000). Classroom language and literacy learning. In M. Kamil, P. D. Pearson, and R. Barr (Eds.), *Handbook of reading research* (Vol. 3, pp. 337–360). Mahweh, NJ: Erlbaum.

Winograd, P., & Hare, V. C. (1988). Direct instruction of reading comprehension strategies: The nature of teacher explanation. In C. E. Weinstein, E. T. Goetz, & P. A. Alexander (Eds.), *Learning and study strategies: Issues in assessment instructional and evaluation* (pp. 121–139). San Diego, CA: Academic Press.

Wolf, M., & Katzir-Cohen, T. (2001). Reading fluency and its intervention. *Scientific Studies of Reading, 5*, 211–239.

Wood, D., Bruner, J. S., & Ross, G. (1976). The role of tutoring in problem solving. *Journal of Child Psychology & Psychiatric & Allied Disciplines, 17*(2), 89–100.

Wood, D., & Middleton, D. (1975). A study of assisted problem-solving. *British Journal of Psychology, 66*(2), 181–191.

Wren, S. (2002). Ten myths of reading comprehension. *SEDL Letter, 14*(3), 3–8.

Xiang, Y., Dahlin, M., Cronin, J., Theaker, R., & Durant, S. (2011). *Do high flyers maintain their altitude? Performance trends of top students.* Washington, DC: Thomas B. Fordham Institute.

Yopp, H. K. (1995). Read-aloud books for developing phonemic awareness: An annotated bibliography. *The Reading Teacher, 48*, 538–542.

Yopp, H. K., & Yopp, R. H. (2000). Supporting phonemic awareness development in the classroom. *The Reading Teacher, 54*(2), 130–143.

Yuen, L. H. F. (2009). From foot to shoes: Kindergartners', families', and teachers' perceptions of the project approach. *Early Childhood Education, 37*, 23–33. doi: 10.1007/s10643–009–0322–3

Zahar, R., Cobb, T., & Spada, N. (2001). Acquiring vocabulary through reading: Effects of frequency and contextual richness. *The Canadian Modern Language Review, 57*(4), 541–572.